BEHAVIOR
Academies

TARGETED INTERVENTIONS THAT WORK!

Jessica Djabrayan Hannigan

John Hannigan

Solution Tree | Press

a division of
Solution Tree

555 North Morton Street
Bloomington, IN 47404
800.733.6786 (toll free) / 812.336.7700
FAX: 812.336.7790

email: info@SolutionTree.com
SolutionTree.com

Visit **go.SolutionTree.com/behavior** to download the free reproducibles in this book.

Visit **go.SolutionTree.com/behavior/BA** and enter the unique access code found on the inside front cover to access the exclusive online reproducibles in this book.

Printed in the United States of America

Library of Congress Cataloging-in-Publication Data

Names: Hannigan, John, author. | Djabrayan Hannigan, Jessica, author.
Title: Behavior academies : targeted interventions that work! / John
   Hannigan, Jessica Djabrayan Hannigan.
Description: Bloomington, IN : Solution Tree Press, [2024] | Includes
   bibliographical references and index.
Identifiers: LCCN 2023049062 (print) | LCCN 2023049063 (ebook) | ISBN
   9781960574084 (paperback) | ISBN 9781960574091 (ebook)
Subjects: LCSH: Behavior modification. | Problem children--Behavior
   modification. | School discipline. | Educational psychology. | School
   improvement programs.
Classification: LCC LB1060.2 .H365 2024 (print) | LCC LB1060.2 (ebook) |
   DDC 371.39/3--dc23/eng/20231206
LC record available at https://lccn.loc.gov/2023049062
LC ebook record available at https://lccn.loc.gov/2023049063

Solution Tree
Jeffrey C. Jones, CEO
Edmund M. Ackerman, President

Solution Tree Press
President and Publisher: Douglas M. Rife
Associate Publishers: Todd Brakke and Kendra Slayton
Editorial Director: Laurel Hecker
Art Director: Rian Anderson
Copy Chief: Jessi Finn
Production Editor: Todd Brakke
Acquisitions Editor: Hilary Goff
Assistant Acquisitions Editor: Elijah Oates
Content Development Specialist: Amy Rubenstein
Associate Editor: Sarah Ludwig
Editorial Assistant: Anne Marie Watkins

This book is dedicated to our son, John E. Hannigan V (aka. John John). Your constant support and encouragement of "you got this mom and dad" motivated every page of this book. May all students benefit from the life skills in this book that will help make this world a better place. This book is a testament to our hope for a world where every child is met with the compassion and guidance they deserve, much like you. May you always feel as supported and loved as the students we wish to reach through these words.

With all our love, Mom and Dad

ACKNOWLEDGMENTS

We wish to personally thank all schools and districts across the United States we have trained to utilize behavior academies. Also, to all of our supervisors, mentors, professors, colleagues, students, friends, and family who have allowed us to innovate and share our passion for what we believe in. This would not have been possible without all of you.

To the Djabrayan and Hannigan families, we thank you for your endless love, support, and encouragement. A special thank you to our parents, Bedros and Dzovinar Djabrayan and Mike and Sky Hannigan, for your help and relentless support during this process.

To our amazing children, John John, Riley, and Rowan, thank you for all your love and support and for always being our number one fans. Through this book, we hope to model for you what it means to set high goals and never give up.

Our appreciation goes out to the exceptional team at Solution Tree (family) for recognizing this is a comprehensive method of addressing and supporting student behaviors. Thank you to Jeffrey C. Jones and Douglas M. Rife for taking the time to learn about our book and giving us the platform to share our voice and help students. Thank you to Claudia Wheatley for being our biggest support and advocate for our work. We extend our gratitude and special appreciation to the following Solution Tree team members who worked tirelessly to help make sure this book was exactly what we envisioned: Todd Brakke, Kendra Slayton, Laurel Hecker, Rian Anderson, Jessi Finn, Sarah Ludwig, and Anne Marie Watkins. We are beyond grateful and proud of this finished product that would not have been possible without your passion and expertise.

A special acknowledgment and thank you to our dear friend, mentor, and colleague Mike Mattos for always guiding and supporting our ideas. Your wisdom and belief in us have been invaluable. Your willingness to share your knowledge, offer guidance, and provide constructive feedback has helped us grow personally and professionally in ways we could never have imagined. But it's not just your professional insights that we cherish; it's the friendship and genuine care you have shown us that have made a profound impact. Your kindness, generosity, and unwavering support have been a constant source of inspiration.

To all who read this book, we thank you for truly doing what is best for all students and having a growth behavior mindset.

Visit **go.SolutionTree.com/behavior** to
download the free reproducibles in this book.

Visit **go.SolutionTree.com/behavior/BA** and enter
the unique access code found on the inside front cover to
access the exclusive online reproducibles in this book.

TABLE OF CONTENTS

Reproducible pages are in italics.

CHAPTER 4

CHAPTER 5

CHAPTER 6

ABOUT THE AUTHORS

 **Jessica Djabrayan Hannigan, EdD,** works with U.S. schools and districts to design and implement effective social-emotional and behavioral systems. Her expertise includes response to intervention (RTI), PLCs, MTSS, PBIS, restorative practices, social-emotional learning, and more.

In addition to her role as an associate professor in the educational leadership department at California State University, Fresno, Dr. Hannigan serves on the California Department of Education design team for the implementation of MTSS to help advocate and change the trending discipline inequity throughout the state's schools and create positive school climates for all students.

The combination of her special education and student support services background, school- and district-level administration, and graduate-level teaching and research experiences has allowed Dr. Hannigan to develop inclusive research-based best practices for systemically implementing equitable behavior initiatives.

Dr. Hannigan has been recognized as the California Outstanding School Psychologist of the Year, as well as other awards from Outstanding Faculty Publications at California State University, Fresno. She was recognized by the California Legislature Assembly for her work in social justice and equity, and she received the inaugural Association of California School Administrators Exemplary Women in Education Award in 2017 for her work on equity in schools.

Dr. Hannigan earned a bachelor's degree in psychology, a master's degree in school psychology, an administrative credential, and a doctorate in educational leadership.

Dr. Hannigan has written numerous articles and coauthored ten bestselling books. She is the cofounder of Hannigan Ed-Equity Group LLC.

To learn more about Dr. Hannigan's work, follow @Jess_hannigan on X, formerly known as Twitter.

John Hannigan, EdD, has served in education for over twenty years as a teacher, instructional coach, principal, and county office leadership coach. John is a sought-after presenter who works with schools and districts throughout North America on designing and implementing systematic multitiered systems of supports for academics and behavior.

During his nine years as principal at Reagan Elementary in the Sanger Unified School District in California, Dr. Hannigan was the leader of a highly effective professional learning community (PLC). He and his staff were recognized as a National Model PLC, California State Distinguished School, Gold Ribbon School, and California Honor Roll School. They also received the Title I Academic Achievement Award and earned Platinum status for positive behavioral interventions and supports (PBIS), in addition to being selected as a knowledge-development site for the statewide scaling up of multitiered systems of supports (MTSS).

Dr. Hannigan has written numerous articles and coauthored ten bestselling books. He is the cofounder of Hannigan Ed-Equity Group LLC.

Dr. Hannigan holds a doctorate in educational leadership from California State University, Fresno.

To learn more about Dr. Hannigan's work, follow @JohnHannigan75 on X, formerly known as Twitter.

To book John Hannigan or Jessica Djabrayan Hannigan for professional development, contact pd@SolutionTree.com.

Building Context

As educators, we entered this profession to help every student become productive, empathic members in our respective communities. This moral impetus that brought us into our profession has become increasingly difficult to sustain given the growing behavior challenges facing our schools and classrooms. More specifically, teachers have cited poor student behavior as their most serious challenge, according to a study of the Joint Legislative Audit and Review Commission (Commonwealth of Virginia, 2022). Over 80 percent of schools report that student behavior has worsened significantly over time (National Center for Education Statistics, 2022). Many of us personally know educators who have left the profession as a result of the challenges of student behavior, or you, personally, may have considered it yourself. Schools are struggling to effectively remedy student behavior as a challenge on their campus.

We know some students need additional time and targeted support to learn and demonstrate appropriate academic and social behaviors to succeed in school and life. We also know there are educators who need practical, meaningful, and proven methods of providing behavior interventions and support. Yet, even with the abundance of ready-made packaged behavior intervention curricula available, we continue to see educators struggle with the understanding (*why*) and implementation (*how*) of targeted behavior interventions that work. We also commonly see educators universally apply a single behavior intervention, such as check-in check-out (CICO), as a catchall intervention, then wonder why students are not effectively responding. CICO is a popular behavior intervention designed for repeated minor classroom misbehaviors and requires frequent positive feedback throughout the day from the assigned educators to help students engage in appropriate targeted behaviors. However, here is what we routinely see as misguided school responses to various other behaviors.

- ▶ **"[Student] can't keep their hands to themselves."** School response: CICO
- ▶ **"[Student] continues to make mean comments to other students."** School response: CICO

> ▸ **"[Student] is bullying other students."** School response: CICO

You can see the pattern.

In addition to the mismatch of CICO for a variety of behaviors, we have also seen the CICO "life sentence," where, for example, a student is placed in CICO during their third-grade year and three years later (now a sixth grader) is still in CICO. We want to be very clear—we do not have any issues or concerns with CICO or any other ready-made behavior interventions; however, we do have concerns with the ways they are misused or overused. Instead, we advocate for behavior interventions to target the specific skills a student is struggling to demonstrate and provide the actual teaching of *replacement behaviors* (life skills) based on the identified academic and social behavior needs. With targeted behavior interventions in place, the responses should instead look as follows.

> ▸ **"[Student] can't keep their hands to themselves."** School response: Hands-Off Academy, where the student will learn impulse-control, self-regulation skills, and so on
>
> ▸ **"[Student] continues to make mean comments to other students."** School response: Civility Academy, where the student will learn empathic listening, perspective taking, compassion skills, and so on
>
> ▸ **"[Student] is bullying other students."** School response: Upstander Academy, where the student will learn self-perception, moral leadership skills, and so on

This is a contrast from a one-size-fits-all school response list where every challenging behavior is matched to one familiar behavior intervention, such as CICO. The preceding list shows the school response for each behavior matched with the appropriate behavior academies (targeted behavior interventions) designed to help students learn new life skills and corresponding replacement behaviors for their targeted area (or areas) of need. The core premise of this book is to provide a practical resource for educators to shift away from a one-size-fits-all approach to behavior intervention by expanding their menu of targeted behavior interventions. The more targeted the reteaching, the more effective the outcomes will be for students.

Let's look at a common school response for a student who struggles with an academic skill such as fluency. When a student struggles with fluency, the school targets exactly which missing skills are impeding this student's fluency and delivers a response of explicit teaching while providing additional time and support to get that student reading fluently. The student may take a phonics screener to identify exactly where fluency is breaking down. The screener may pinpoint that the student hasn't mastered all vowel blends and digraphs; the school then provides targeted instruction for the student to learn the skills of vowel blends and digraphs to begin reading fluently.

When it comes to behavior, however, schools don't typically target the skills the student is struggling with that are contributing to the behaviors he or she is demonstrating, then teach those skills so there is a reduction or elimination of those behaviors. The response is typically through repeated punishments and the use of exclusionary practices in an attempt to change a student's behavior and/or assigning the common CICO. We wanted to know why this exists and to provide a practical resource to shift from this typical response.

Barriers to Behavior Intervention Implementation

We surveyed thousands of educators across the nation on what their challenges are in implementing behavior interventions at their school. We analyzed their responses and grouped them into the factors and related challenges indicated in table I.1. This table identifies some of the most common behavior intervention implementation factors and related challenges.

TABLE I.1: Common Behavior Intervention Implementation Factors and Related Challenges

Factor	Related Challenge
Time	"We don't have time to provide them."
Lack of capacity	"We do not know how to implement."
Limited human resources	"We do not have the people who can provide this level of support. I only have a counselor one day a week."
Scheduling	"There is no room in the schedule."
Need for behavior intervention curriculum	"We don't know what to use to teach the students. Are we supposed to create these lessons on our own?"
Limited training	"I didn't go to school for this."
Unclear roles and responsibilities	"This is not my job; it is your job."
Effectiveness not measured	"We do not monitor to see if what we are doing is working."
Lack of schoolwide and classwide prevention systems in place	"We have too many kids who need interventions."
Fixed beliefs about student behavior	"These students cannot learn new behaviors. This is a waste of time."

Do any of these behavior intervention implementation factors and related challenges sound familiar? If so, this is why we wrote this book. Specifically, we want to help make implementing behavior interventions effective, less complicated, and easier to do. Our two main outcomes of this book are to (1) help educators understand the thinking and structure behind effective targeted behavior interventions and (2) help educators implement practical, easy-to-do behavior interventions that work. Behavior academies are the vehicle to achieve both outcomes. However, there are two presuppositions that we often see schools struggle with that create barriers to successfully implementing behavior academies.

The first supposition is that only the school behavior specialists can deliver a behavior academy. We acknowledge only a small number of educators within a school or district system have additional schooling as part of their college degree and credentialing where they learned how to design and implement behavior interventions. Even those who specifically specialized and majored in behavior may have learned the theory behind how to develop behavior interventions but need assistance to systematize implementation across a school setting. We also recognize most teachers and school administrators may have had only one formal course, if any, during teacher or administrator preparation programs on classroom or schoolwide behavior in general. If you were like most educators, you received the keys to your classroom and the Harry and Rosemary T. Wong (2018) book, *The First Days of School*, and off you went. We recognize there will be a range of learning for some more than others around implementing targeted behavior interventions such as behavior academies, and that is OK. The practical approach we outline in this book will make implementing behavior academies doable for any educator, regardless of behavior expertise and training. We provide a range of application uses later in this book to give options for educators on formalized and informalized ways of using this resource.

The second supposition is for schools to jump straight into intervention as a way to "fix the bad students," a quote we hear often from educators without having any Tier 1 schoolwide prevention in place on their campus or in classrooms for behavior. No behavior intervention exists that will replace the impact of true systematic tiers of behavior supports, also referred to as response to intervention (RTI) and (often used interchangeably) as multitiered system of supports (MTSS) specifically. In our book, *Behavior Solutions: Teaching Academic and Social Skills Through RTI at Work* (Hannigan, Hannigan, Mattos, & Buffum, 2021), we help educators develop and implement a multitiered approach (RTI or MTSS) for behavior that is worth referencing if you are interested in creating the overall system for behavior at your school. Simply put, if half the students in your school need behavior interventions, you'll need to address Tier 1 prevention schoolwide and classwide because your school does not have an intervention problem.

You can utilize this book as a companion to *Behavior Solutions* to expand on schoolwide systematic development of behavior interventions or as a stand-alone resource for anyone just interested in implementing behavior academies (targeted behavior interventions) to help students learn productive replacement behaviors. However, we must be specific in noting that the absence of prevention on your campus will leave you with too many students needing a behavior academy, thus leading to less effective outcomes for students.

Thinking Behind Behavior Academies—Skills for Life

Can we agree that even as adults, we have had experiences in our lives requiring us to learn and practice new life skills to successfully navigate through academic and social situations? Specifically, have you had to learn and practice life skills that help you do the following?

- ▸ Identify and respond appropriately when you are triggered.
- ▸ Problem solve.
- ▸ Stay organized.
- ▸ Improve self-confidence.
- ▸ Have effective time management.
- ▸ Communicate effectively with others, written or verbally.
- ▸ Ask for help.
- ▸ Identify and make sense of your emotions.
- ▸ Stand up for yourself.
- ▸ Stay motivated.
- ▸ Persevere during tough times.
- ▸ Set goals.
- ▸ Be resilient.
- ▸ Set boundaries.
- ▸ Be nice.
- ▸ Navigate through jealous feelings or emotions.
- ▸ Give yourself grace.
- ▸ Coexist.
- ▸ Have difficult conversations.
- ▸ Self-reflect.
- ▸ Navigate feelings of isolation or rejection.
- ▸ Understand someone else's perspective.
- ▸ Make and keep friends.
- ▸ Respond to feeling anxious or overwhelmed.
- ▸ Work through feeling down or helpless.
- ▸ Struggle maintaining healthy relationships.
- ▸ Not give up easily.

We are fairly confident your answer is *yes*. The majority of adults are constantly working on life skills that eventually become productive habits. If we as adults are continually working on these life skills to navigate work and life, of course students whose brains are still developing will also need support and practice applying these life skills when they need them; hence, the thinking behind behavior academies. Not only do we need to know what targeted life skills students need help developing into productive habits, but we as educators must also help *teach* them replacement behaviors so they can demonstrate the targeted life skills in various situations. It is one thing to identify targeted life skills students need; it is another to actually teach them the "how to" knowledge necessary to demonstrate those identified targeted life skills. Simply put, we are building their inner toolkit of replacement behaviors to draw from whether we are in their presence or not and providing opportunities to *apply* their learning in a safe space. Behavior academies do just that.

Behavior academies are developed from the research on establishing productive habits and the power of utilizing behavior rehearsals to practice and generalize new targeted life skills using imagery and visualization exercises (which we will explain in depth in chapter 3). *Productive habits* (the appropriate life skills that occur automatically when students respond to everyday academic and social behavior situations) do not form overnight. In fact, some of the most current research on establishing productive habits reveals the median for human beings to establish an automatic habit is, on average, sixty-six days (Clear, 2018). Establishing productive habits by teaching *targeted life skills* and the corresponding replacement behaviors while giving students opportunities to *practice* (rehearse) them is rooted in the design of our behavior academies. In fact, this book will help students learn a variety of targeted life skills that can be stacked or built upon within their personal toolkits. We want to help students develop an inner toolkit of life skills they can access and utilize automatically in school and career.

To begin building the context for behavior academies, we ask the following two questions to educators.

1. What are the challenging academic and social behaviors you are seeing from your students?

2. What targeted life skills do you think your students may be struggling with?

Oftentimes, educators can list the challenging behaviors with relative ease; however, it becomes much more difficult to identify the targeted life skills those particular students may need additional help with that are contributing to the challenging behavior they just listed. For example, a student demonstrating apathetic behavior may indicate a need for additional targeted support and practice in the area of developing a good self-concept, a student shutting down easily may demonstrate a need for support in identifying emotions and having the appropriate replacement behaviors to respond, and so on. To help visualize the connection between behavior and targeted life skills, we listed some of these responses in table I.2.

Effective responses to these two questions requires educators to shift from traditional beliefs and practices regarding challenging student behaviors. Specifically, the process of answering the two questions allows educators to shift their thinking from the focus on challenging behaviors toward the focus on the targeted *life skill needs* of the students. If we look at challenging behaviors as a form of communication of needs, then we are empowered with evidence to take action to support students with those identified targeted areas. As a result, educators need to identify areas of need for the students and use behavior academies as a vehicle to help build on student strengths while providing replacement behaviors in these specific targeted areas of need. In this book, we simplify the process by providing a behavior academy structure and ready-made behavior academies inclusive of targeted student needs.

TABLE I.2: Connections Between Behaviors and Life Skills

What are the challenging academic or social behaviors you are seeing?	What targeted life skills do you think students may be struggling with?
Apathy	Self-concept
Lack of engagement	Self-discipline
Silent	Self-confidence
Disruptive	Impulse control
Lack of focus	Goal setting
Opposition	Solving problems
Attention seeking	Relationship building
Peer attention	Social awareness
Shutting down	Identifying emotions
Lack of motivation	Self-motivation
Anger	Self-regulation
Staying organized	Prioritizing
Giving up easily	Self-efficacy

About This Book

We wrote this book with students in mind first and foremost. We wanted to make sure educators had the tools needed to continue helping students learn and develop productive life skills (additional tools in their inner toolkit) to help them with school and life. We provide educators with a range of application options for how to utilize behavior academies. Whether you are a school administrator, behavior intervention team member, classroom teacher, school counselor, school psychologist, school social worker, or even parent or guardian, you will find the thinking and resources behind behavior academies beneficial regardless of how formalized or informalized you decide to implement them. We wrote this book in a manner that allows you to decide what level of implementation will be the best fit for students. We provide a formalized behavior intervention structure (behavior academies structure) that intervention team members can use, but we also provide additional informal ways of utilizing the resources to help teachers support their students and even support parents or guardians at home.

Let's take a look at what you'll find in the chapters that follow. In chapter 1 (page 9), you receive the opportunity to explore and self-reflect on the behavior mindset necessary for the successful implementation of behavior academies. In chapter 2 (page 19), we define behavior academies to ensure you have a common definition and common understanding of behavior academies. In chapter 3 (page 25), you learn about the behavior academy structure to help with the most formalized level of implementation. This chapter outlines the thinking and intended design for behavior academy implementation, along with helpful tools to guide implementation. In chapter 4 (page 57), you'll find the behavior rehearsal cards from all eight behavior academies. Essentially, each behavior rehearsal card is a ready-made behavior academy session for any educator, parent, or guardian. In chapter 5 (page 131), you learn how to build your own behavior academy. This chapter is designed to walk you through one phase at a time of building your behavior academy with samples to guide your learning. In chapter 6 (page 141), you get the answers to frequently asked questions about behavior academies. This will help educators navigate through how to implement them effectively. Our epilogue (page 159) offers conclusions and encouraging words as you take your next steps forward with implementation. Finally, a closing appendix (page 161) includes reproducible versions of the many tools shown across this book's chapters.

Chapter 1

Behavior Mindset

Before we discuss behavior academies in detail in chapter 2 (page 19), we feel it's necessary to address the behavior mindset of the adults. We find that the leading indicator of behavior intervention implementation success (that is, the implementation of behavior academies) correlates highly with the belief mindset of the adults providing the additional time and targeted behavior support to students. Imagine implementing something you do not believe will work. Where would you find the motivation and drive to continue being relentless if a student experiences setbacks or if the implementation takes longer than you imagined? If the educators do not have a supportive behavior mindset about student behavior, we can assure you that the students will (1) see right through the disingenuous adult actions, and (2) implementation will fail.

This chapter highlights what it looks like when behavior mindsets are inconsistent with the goals and outcomes of behavior academies and how such mindsets act as a poison pill for the work. We contrast this with how a productive behavior mindset positively influences all behavior interventions. Finally, we introduce and provide a behavior mindset self-inventory to help with self-reflection and to ensure the mindsets of the adults providing or supporting behavior academies are consistent with the goals of the behavior academies.

Unproductive (*Fixed*) Behavior Mindset

Let us share an experience we had while writing this book to highlight implementation red flags, an unproductive (*fixed*) behavior mindset in action. A *fixed mindset*, as defined by Dweck (2017), is the belief that all qualities are innate and unchangeable, a belief we expand on by focusing on student behaviors. Fittingly, we refer to an unproductive (*fixed*) behavior mindset as the belief that *student behaviors* are innate and unchangeable. Such mindsets block an educator's ability to own and invest in the ongoing teaching of targeted life skills and corresponding replacement behaviors.

Allow us to share an experience we had with a school to demonstrate what we mean by unproductive (*fixed*) behavior mindset. We had the opportunity to observe a "not quite there yet" behavior intervention team meeting with a group of educators responsible for providing the targeted behavior interventions at this school. The purpose of this team was to work collaboratively to ensure all students who need additional time and targeted behavior support receive it. This team was comprised of two administrators, one full-time counselor, one part-time social worker (on-site two days a week), one part-time school psychologist (on-site three days a week, but primarily utilized for special education testing and crisis), and one full-time MTSS behavior lead (teacher on special assignment due to her experience with behavior)—a number of support staff most schools would envy. As a response to the harmful impact the pandemic has had on the mental health of students, this district placed an increased focus on mental health and behavior support by increasing staffing to aid the implementation of behavior interventions.

Unfortunately, the behavior intervention team was not seeing the results it had expected with the addition of these supports, and the reason was due to the collective unproductive (*fixed*) behavior mindset of the educators charged with leading this work (including the administration). It was as if the more resources they were given, the further they were from implementing effective behavior interventions. For each new position created, the prior lead would delegate their responsibilities onto that new person. They were playing the "tag, you're it" game and creating more excuses than actions for why they could not implement behavior interventions.

The energy we observed in the room during the meeting was negative; some members casually walked in late and appeared bothered about even having to attend. We could feel the tension just sitting there. Some members were group texting each other while others were talking or answering emails. Negative comments were being made about students without anyone (including the administration) addressing that this is not how we speak about students. No amount of resources can be allocated to solve a problem where such a toxic culture and mindset exists. The unproductive (*fixed*) mindset around student behavior (and in this case, from the people specifically hired to help in this area) quickly became an infectious collective unproductive (*fixed*) mindset that spread among this behavior intervention team and, ultimately, across its school staff.

Additionally, not one member on the behavior intervention team could share an actual formalized behavior intervention they were offering for the students who needed them the most; when asked about it, they were very defensive. For example, when each behavior intervention team member was asked to provide an update on the behavior interventions they delivered and how the effectiveness of the interventions were measured, it was met with excuses and a list of interactions (such as quick student check-ins, calling home, making a referral for outside-of-school supports, holding additional student success team meetings to discuss further, and so on) rather than actual ongoing behavior interventions (such as behavior academies). Additionally, evidence of effectiveness of what they were currently doing to support students was based more on emotion rather than actual student data. One of the team members even said in regard to a student not responding to what they were providing, "That kid just takes up oxygen anyway."

Unfortunately, these types of comments about students seemed like a natural occurrence in these behavior intervention team meetings. We knew in this case, and many similar cases, the only way to see positive student outcomes would be to have honest and accountable conversations about behavior—adult *and* student behavior, and specifically, behavior mindset.

We have also had to navigate through the "we are already doing it"–isms in other cases. This is a phenomenon where educators claim they are implementing behavior interventions without evidence of implementation or data to demonstrate effectiveness, and the students take the blame for not responding to what they are providing. While this unproductive (*fixed*) mindset is not as outwardly toxic as the prior example, it is indeed unproductive. This is a difficult place to be as a behavior intervention team or an individual educator attempting behavior interventions because how can educators grow individually or collectively as a team if they already believe their intervention practices are solid and the reason students are not responding effectively is a direct manifestation of the students themselves? Behavior mindset shifts do not happen overnight; they require intentionality and evidence of effective student outcomes to help change beliefs. The preceding are just two examples of how contagious an unproductive (*fixed*) behavior mindset outcome can be.

We have also witnessed individual educators' (*fixed*) behavior mindset in other capacities negatively impact the implementation of behavior academies. For example, we have seen situations where a student enrolled in a behavior academy with a counselor to work on emotional regulation targeted life skills and corresponding replacement behaviors, but the teacher who is supposed to help reinforce and encourage the application of these newly learned targeted life skills and corresponding replacement behaviors thinks it is a waste of time and will not work to help the student. Moreover, a teacher may not understand the targeted focus of the behavior academy and therefore fail to recognize growth in student behavior in that particular targeted area of focus. This way of thinking and behaving will have to be disrupted for behavior academies to work.

Productive (*Growth*) Behavior Mindset

In contrast to an unproductive (*fixed*) mindset, Dweck (2017) defines a *growth mindset* as the belief that even through challenges and setbacks, people can grow and improve new skills over time if they work at it. We refer to a productive (*growth*) behavior mindset as the belief that *student behaviors* can be improved by the teaching of targeted life skills and corresponding replacement behaviors. We want to provide two examples of what we mean by a productive (*growth*) behavior mindset: one of a collective group and the other of an individual teacher.

First, we observed a behavior intervention team quite the opposite of the previous one described and with far fewer staffing resources. This behavior intervention team was made up of one administrator, one full-time counselor, a teacher on special assignment for behavior, and a behavior aid. From the beginning of the meeting, it was evident the behavior intervention team knew their purpose and their *why* to help students who needed targeted behavior interventions. They started the meeting with a brief check-in and then began discussing each of the formalized behavior interventions they led. For example, the counselor began by presenting how many students she currently had in her two targeted behavior academies (a Hands-Off Academy and an Upstander Academy) as well as how the students were responding with the use of data aligned with their behavior academy goals. She was open to ongoing suggestions from the team for any students who were not yet meeting their goals. Next, the teacher on special assignment for behavior shared how well CICO was going for the five students receiving it. She suggested adding a CICO academy to the traditional CICO procedures to ensure students were being provided with some targeted life skills and their corresponding replacement behaviors to help them meet their classroom CICO goals. The team believed this was a great idea, and the teacher on special assignment for behavior said she would take the lead on ensuring that weekly CICO behavior academy sessions were delivered starting the following week. The behavior aid also shared an update on how she was supporting the students receiving behavior interventions during unstructured times and how she was helping them reinforce their newly learned targeted life skills and corresponding replacement behaviors. The administration provided input and support throughout the meeting.

As a behavior intervention team, this group was focused on problem solving (being productive) rather than making excuses or blaming students. Overall, the meeting was positive and effective. The members of the team were also vulnerable to areas they had to improve as the leads delivering the behavior interventions, such as improving teacher communication, adjusting behavior goals, strengthening parent and guardian partnerships, and ensuring proper reinforcements were in place for students. Most importantly, they used student data to guide how they would continue to improve as a behavior intervention team each time they met. This was a stark difference from the collective unproductive (*fixed*) behavior mindset example we provided earlier. In this example, there was a collective productive (*growth*) behavior mindset, which was contagious to the members on the behavior intervention team and the other school staff supporting implementation.

We have also witnessed individual educators' productive (*growth*) behavior mindset in other capacities that have impacted the implementation of behavior academies. For example, we spoke to a teacher whose student was in a Hands-Off Academy. She shared how much the work of the counselor has helped her student learn new targeted life skills and corresponding replacement behaviors. She shared that after each behavior academy session, the counselor provided her with an update on what skills were worked on with the student so she could help reinforce and celebrate the wins when observing the student using these newly learned skills. Again, this is a huge contrast from the previous scenario of a teacher believing behavior academies are a waste of time and not focusing on the targeted area of need to support the student. Another individual teacher we spoke to shared how she loves the thinking behind behavior academies so much that she started implementing them in a more informalized fashion once a week with her entire class and noticed huge growth overall in her targeted area of focus, which was improving social skills.

Now that you have seen examples of both unproductive (*fixed*) and productive (*growth*) behavior mindsets, you can conceptualize evidence of either mindset present that would support or impede the effective implementation of behavior academies. Use the behavior mindset self-inventory introduced in the next section as a self-reflection tool and first step on your journey toward successful implementation of behavior academies. This tool can necessitate the dialogue needed to confront barriers by reflecting inward prior to creating and implementing targeted behavior academies. Specifically, this behavior mindset self-inventory helps capture some of the characteristics of unproductive (*fixed*) behavior mindset and productive (*growth*) behavior mindset.

Behavior Mindset Self-Inventory

The behavior mindset self-inventory was designed for the purpose of helping educators identify their current behavior mindset. Specifically, the behavior mindset self-inventory provides educators with a look into their individual assumptions about student behavior. Taking the time to self-reflect in an honest fashion is the start of shifting from a fixed to a growth mindset around behavior. If an educator does not have the self-awareness that they are demonstrating a fixed mindset (through their actions or comments about student behavior), it will be difficult for them to see the reasons for an alternative approach to student behavior support. The behavior mindset self-inventory statements are derived from an analysis of over a thousand educator responses across all grade levels throughout the United States and a range of differences between unproductive (*fixed*) and productive (*growth*) behavior mindsets. The following sections provide answers to common questions about this self-inventory.

Who Is the Behavior Mindset Self-Inventory For?

Because self-inventories act as a reflection tool, any educators who help support student academic or social behaviors (or both) can benefit from them. This includes but is not limited to teachers, counselors, psychologists, social workers, administrators, and any other behavior support staff.

Why Does the Behavior Mindset Self-Inventory Matter to Me?

We have found through our research and work with practitioners that the primary reason behavior interventions do not work is the unproductive (*fixed*) behavior mindset of the educators providing them. If the educators do not have a productive (*growth*) behavior mindset, they (1) will implement the behavior interventions ineffectively and (2) cannot justify the importance of implementing them to themselves or others, which will result in implementation failure. This behavior mindset self-reflection tool will help you confront the barriers (unproductive beliefs) that will hinder implementation.

What Is Your Current Mindset About Behavior?

To assess your current mindset about behavior, review the statements and rate yourself on your behavior mindset. Please be honest in your responses. This self-inventory can be used anonymously as an individual self-check or collectively as a group self-check to assess the beliefs of all stakeholders implementing the behavior interventions (see figure 1.1). (See page 162 for a reproducible version of this figure.) Remember, its design is to serve as a self-reflection and self-awareness of where you currently stand in your mindset about behavior.

1. Students should be punished when not demonstrating appropriate behaviors.

1	2	3	4	5
Strongly Disagree	Disagree	Neutral	Agree	Strongly Agree

2. Student behavior should be viewed as the communication of unmet needs and the absence of developed life skills and not taken personally.

1	2	3	4	5
Strongly Disagree	Disagree	Neutral	Agree	Strongly Agree

3. Someone other than myself should be teaching students appropriate behaviors (that is, their parents, school specialists, administrator, additional special services, and so on).

1	2	3	4	5
Strongly Disagree	Disagree	Neutral	Agree	Strongly Agree

4. Students need additional time and targeted support to learn appropriate replacement behaviors and receive opportunities to practice and generalize them.

1	2	3	4	5
Strongly Disagree	Disagree	Neutral	Agree	Strongly Agree

5. Exclusionary practices (that is, detention, suspensions, Saturday school, expulsions) will help improve a student's behavior.

1	2	3	4	5
Strongly Disagree	Disagree	Neutral	Agree	Strongly Agree

6. Students' behavior and life skills are developed over time with proper support.

1	2	3	4	5
Strongly Disagree	Disagree	Neutral	Agree	Strongly Agree

7. Student behavior is innate; therefore, additional targeted time, support, and practice will have a modest impact to improve their outcomes.

1	2	3	4	5
Strongly Disagree	Disagree	Neutral	Agree	Strongly Agree

8. Behavior interventions should provide targeted teaching and support of specific life skills.

1	2	3	4	5
Strongly Disagree	Disagree	Neutral	Agree	Strongly Agree

9. If student behavior doesn't improve right away, I feel frustrated and blame the intervention for being ineffective.

1	2	3	4	5
Strongly Disagree	Disagree	Neutral	Agree	Strongly Agree

10. I know improvement takes time, and I celebrate small wins with a student's behavior.

1	2	3	4	5
Strongly Disagree	Disagree	Neutral	Agree	Strongly Agree

11. I do not have time to teach or reteach students appropriate behavior.

1	2	3	4	5
Strongly Disagree	Disagree	Neutral	Agree	Strongly Agree

12. Ongoing feedback and support are critical to help with improving a student's behavior.

1	2	3	4	5
Strongly Disagree	Disagree	Neutral	Agree	Strongly Agree

13. Ongoing updates on a student's behavior progress are not important to me.

1	2	3	4	5
Strongly Disagree	Disagree	Neutral	Agree	Strongly Agree

14. I embrace the challenge of helping students learn appropriate behaviors.

1	2	3	4	5
Strongly Disagree	Disagree	Neutral	Agree	Strongly Agree

15. The majority of students receiving additional behavior interventions will not successfully respond to these supports at my school.

1	2	3	4	5
Strongly Disagree	Disagree	Neutral	Agree	Strongly Agree

FIGURE 1.1: Behavior mindset self-inventory.

continued →

16. At our school, we take collective responsibility for supporting a student's behavioral needs.

1	2	3	4	5
Strongly Disagree	Disagree	Neutral	Agree	Strongly Agree

17. There needs to be a special behavior program, classroom, or school within our district to which to send students who need extra help with behavior that provides the necessary time and space for them to learn.

1	2	3	4	5
Strongly Disagree	Disagree	Neutral	Agree	Strongly Agree

18. Setting realistic goals, progress monitoring them, and working through temporary student setbacks are essential to help improve academic behaviors, social behaviors, or both.

1	2	3	4	5
Strongly Disagree	Disagree	Neutral	Agree	Strongly Agree

19. There is no need to set goals or progress monitor since students will likely give up when they have a setback.

1	2	3	4	5
Strongly Disagree	Disagree	Neutral	Agree	Strongly Agree

20. Student voice is vital to improving student behavior.

1	2	3	4	5
Strongly Disagree	Disagree	Neutral	Agree	Strongly Agree

Behavior Mindset Self-Inventory Scoring

Total from odd numbers: _____   **Total from even numbers:** _____

Unproductive behavior mindset: Total from odd numbers in the 40- to 50-point range and total from even numbers in the 10- to 20-point range

An unproductive behavior mindset is a fixed mindset about student behavior. This type of educator believes students should already know how to demonstrate appropriate academic behaviors, social behaviors, or both. This educator believes that behavior is innate and that students would respond better through punishment than teaching. The unproductive mindset also believes that interventions are not worth the time or that it is the job of others to "fix" the student's behavior.

Undetermined behavior mindset: Total from odd numbers in the 21- to 39-point range and total from even numbers in the 21- to 39-point range

An undetermined behavior mindset is inconsistent beliefs about behavior. This type of educator believes some students can be taught appropriate academic behaviors, social behaviors, or both, and others cannot. While they may feel it is worth investing the time to support some students with their behavior, it should be someone else's job to provide it.

Productive behavior mindset: Total from odd numbers in the 10- to 20-point range and total from even numbers in the 40- to 50-point range

A productive behavior mindset is a growth mindset about student behavior. This type of educator believes that behavior is the communication of unmet needs and additional time, and targeted support will help students demonstrate and generalize appropriate academic behavior, social behavior, or both. This educator believes that behavior can be improved, and it is the collective responsibility of the school to provide the necessary support to ensure every student succeeds.

Scoring note: If the combination of your odd and even scoring ranges does not fall into a behavior mindset category, please consider the following: (1) retake the inventory to make sure you are not contradicting yourself in your ratings, or (2) consider yourself in the undetermined range due to the similarity of your scores supporting both productive and unproductive behavior mindset beliefs.

We thank you for taking a few minutes to self-reflect with the behavior mindset self-inventory. We understand behavior requires a lot of time and energy and is often met with a different emotional reaction than a student struggling with academic content, such as reading. A productive behavior mindset requires the adults who serve students to have positive beliefs about their ability to learn and demonstrate appropriate behaviors. If the adults do not believe students can learn and grow in their behavior, it will be a tough road to maintain the constructive beliefs and relentlessness necessary to continue supporting the students on your campus in greatest need of caring adults who believe in them. This is especially true when students demonstrate behavior setbacks on their journey or when you don't see immediate results.

When educators providing these supports have an unproductive behavior mindset about students, it will become a self-fulfilling prophecy—where obstacles will be met with "I told you so," time invested will be met with "time wasted," pushback from staff will be met with "The district office told us we had to do this," and the lack of a school-wide prevention system will be met with "We have too many students who need this."

Do you believe that the apathetic student refusing to work in class is capable of demonstrating enthusiasm and interest in school? Do you believe that the student showing disrespect to the adults on your campus is capable of being respectful? If you can't honestly answer *yes* to these questions, you will struggle to accept and align your practice to the proven guidance found in the ensuing chapters in this book.

Educators have to believe students can learn new life skills that will one day become productive habits with additional time and targeted behavior support. Educators can decide through their beliefs that become behaviors: Is implementing behavior interventions (such as behavior academies) a task on a compliance checklist or a relentless pursuit to teach the targeted life skills necessary for students to demonstrate prosocial behaviors to thrive in school and life?

In chapter 2, you will learn about the evolution and definition of behavior academies.

Chapter 2

Behavior Academy

An interaction is not an intervention.

—Jessica and John Hannigan

Sometimes, educators conflate an interaction with an intervention and, therefore, are convinced they are doing an intervention. We often hear, "Well, I checked in with him; he's good," "I called him in, and we talked about what he needs to do," or "We tried it for a few days, and it didn't work." Checking in with students in itself is an interaction and not a replacement for a true comprehensive and targeted ongoing behavior intervention. Do not misinterpret what we are saying. Interactions with students are not bad; they are, in fact, positive for the students you support. However, an interaction in itself does not replace an actual targeted, ongoing behavior intervention where students are taught or retaught and given opportunities to generalize and establish new productive habits that will help them in school and life.

Simply put, behavior interventions need to include the *teaching of behavior*. One way we know this can happen intentionally is by implementing behavior academies, an evidenced-based behavior intervention focused on teaching and/or reteaching targeted life skills and their corresponding replacement behaviors.

What Is a Behavior Academy?

Allow us to share how behavior academies originated. Our first behavior academy was unintentionally born in 2010 when a couple of boys with a history of repeated hands-on behavior incidents were involved in a fight in the school restroom while several other students recorded the event—during bully prevention week. Yes, this happened *during* bully prevention week! After reviewing the log entries in these boys' discipline files, it was evident the traditional three- to five-day suspension, which they had received after previous incidents for similar hands-on behavior, had proven to be ineffective. It was also evident that their automatic go-to response when upset or angry was to use their hands through physical aggression instead of healthier life skills to resolve conflict peacefully.

We knew we had two choices: (1) continue using the same ineffective exclusionary practices such as suspension and hope that, through simple maturation, these boys would "grow out of" these behaviors, or (2) use this incident to teach and practice new ways to appropriately respond so these negative behaviors would not repeat in the future. We decided to try the second option.

We called our first behavior academy the *Hands-Off Academy*. The hands-off part of the name came from the targeted area of focus: in this case, hands-off behaviors. The academy component was created to intentionally capture the *ongoing* training and teaching of skills students needed in the identified targeted area of need. So, we called it a Hands-Off Academy because this was not going to be a one-time teaching opportunity but rather a series of teaching opportunities to help students learn and generalize new, effective, and healthier life skills to utilize when they were upset or angry. In addition to the series of targeted behavior lessons, the students had to set goals for themselves and self-monitor their progress toward their propensity to generalize these newly learned life skills with adult support. Adding these intentional layers and ongoing support began to result in improved behaviors from the two boys.

Once we saw how successfully our students responded to our initial Hands-Off Academy, we expanded the thinking across the wide variety of behaviors students were demonstrating on our campus. We also found implementing behavior academies with fidelity proved to reduce discipline *recidivism rates* (students engaging in similar behaviors again); improve student, teacher, and staff behavior perception reports of impact; improve relationships and connections with students; and ultimately, shift a school culture toward a growth behavior mindset.

In its most straightforward form, we define a *behavior academy* as a systematic process to provide additional time, ongoing teaching and/or reteaching support, and rehearsal opportunities for appropriate targeted life skills that can be generalized and developed into productive habits. We have included eight of our most popular behavior academies in this book. These are the behavior academies that are the most requested based on student needs across the United States. See the brief definitions of each in table 2.1.

Each of our behavior academies is named to capture the overall behavior focus.

What Are Targeted Life Skills?

The level of *targetedness* is a crucial part of making a behavior academy intentional and effective. So, identifying the targeted life skills a student is struggling with (which is why the student is demonstrating the behaviors you are seeing) is a critical first step to matching students to the appropriate behavior academy. Refer to table I.2 to review the list of challenging academic and social behaviors we commonly see and possible life skills those students are struggling with. To put this in context, for example, in order to improve hands-off behavior, we need to teach and allow students to practice and apply the targeted life skills that match the appropriate behaviors we are working toward: impulse control, identifying emotional triggers, self-regulation, and so on.

TABLE 2.1: Definitions of Eight Behavior Academies

Academy Type	Academy Purpose
Hands-Off Academy	Designed to help students struggling to keep their hands to themselves when they are angry or perceive a situation to be unfair
Check-In Check-Out Academy	Designed for students struggling with repeated minor classroom misbehaviors
Civility Academy	Designed for students struggling to maintain civil discourse with other peers or adults who may have different points of view
Organizational Skills Academy	Designed for students struggling with organizational skills impacting readiness to learn and work completion
Social Skills Academy	Designed for students struggling with appropriate peer or adult interactions
Upstander Academy	Designed for students demonstrating or participating in bullying-type behaviors
Motivation Academy	Designed for students who appear apathetic toward incomplete work, grades, being in class on time, and so on
Emotional Regulation Academy	Designed for students who are struggling with emotions impacting learning (for example, shutdowns, eloping, emotional outbursts)

Each behavior academy includes eight targeted life skills related to their respective academy. Specifically, for each targeted life skill, students are taught at least one or two replacement behaviors to help them demonstrate the life skill and, most importantly, add additional tools to their inner toolkits. If we were to capture this in an equation format, it would look as follows.

8 targeted life skills + 2 replacement behaviors each = 1 behavior academy

We not only provide eight targeted life skills for *each* of the eight behavior academies in this book (sixty-four targeted life skills to be exact); we also provide what students can do (two replacement behaviors) to help them demonstrate each targeted life skill, totaling 128 replacement behaviors educators can draw from to help students develop them into productive habits.

We want to explain why we selected eight targeted life skills for each behavior academy and why we recommend a skill a week for at least six to eight weeks. Typically, a reasonable timeframe to implement and assess the effectiveness of a behavior intervention is six to eight weeks. This allows for ongoing implementation and the collection of student data points aligned with the goal of the behavior intervention to help you decide if the student is generalizing learned life skills. This suggested timeframe is aligned with the research behind forming new productive habits by Clear (2018), which we mentioned previously—it takes sixty-six days (approximately eight weeks) before newly learned behaviors become automatic (internalized). This is why we selected eight targeted life skills to focus on per each behavior academy. This does not mean we stop an intervention because we are in the eighth week. We stop an intervention when students have demonstrated mastery in their area of need.

An educator can also revisit targeted life skills if they are beyond the eight-week mark or increase the frequency to twice a week if the student is not improving. An educator can add additional or different targeted life skills to focus on, but the main point is for the behavior academy to improve the behavior that made this student a perfect candidate for the specific academy in the first place. Table 2.2 illustrates each of our behavior academies, along with their eight targeted life skills as a reference. We identified these targeted life skills based on our collective experience implementing behavior academies in schools across the United States. As mentioned previously, they do not represent the only possible targeted life skills a student can work on. However, the eight we list here for each behavior academy should serve to model the level of targetedness required to be effective in teaching new targeted life skills aligned to the behaviors students are demonstrating.

TABLE 2.2: Behavior Academies and Targeted Life Skills

Behavior Academy	Targeted Life Skills
Hands-Off Academy	Self-reflection Impulse control Identifying emotional triggers Self-regulation Conflict resolution Accountability Help seeking Communication (verbal and nonverbal)
Check-In Check-Out Academy	Respect for others Active listening Self-control Self-discipline Receptive to feedback Self-monitoring Persistence Responsible decision making
Civility Academy	Empathic listening Integrity Responsibility Social and cultural awareness Coexisting Open minded Perspective taking Compassion

Behavior Academy	Targeted Life Skills
Organizational Skills Academy	Stress management Preparedness Resourceful Flexibility Goal setting Prioritizing Initiative Self-management
Social Skills Academy	Social awareness Self-awareness Turn taking Empathy Cooperation Relationship building Communication (verbal and nonverbal) Patience
Upstander Academy	Self-perception Empathy Action oriented Analyzing situations Self-confidence Digital citizenship Moral leadership Problem solving
Motivation Academy	Self-efficacy Growth mindset Self-monitoring Punctuality Dependable Self-advocacy Goal setting Self-concept
Emotional Regulation Academy	Emotional expression Self-awareness Self-regulation Mindfulness Help seeking Coping Emotional literacy Resilience

In chapter 3, you will learn the behavior academy structure to organize all components necessary for an effective behavior academy delivery.

Behavior Academy Structure

The secret of getting ahead is getting started. The secret of getting started is breaking your complex overwhelming tasks into small manageable tasks, and then starting on the first one.

—Mark Twain

You are probably thinking, "These targeted behavior academies sound great, but where do we start?" As former school administrators, we both know the complexity of setting up an effective system to ensure students receive additional time and targeted support for behavior. Also, as a former classroom teacher and school psychologist, we know there are hundreds of moving parts within a classroom's instructional day and across your school's bell schedule, making it difficult and overwhelming to think about how to provide behavior interventions that work. As mentioned in the introduction (page 1), we acknowledge there are ready-made behavior intervention curricula widely available in many schools, yet implementation continues to be a struggle for many.

We believe we know why this dilemma exists. Similar to having a ready-made academic curriculum handed to teachers without explaining the thinking behind it, the purpose for it, or its design to improve student outcomes, it will create the feeling of a compliance task rather than a tool of support. We wanted to create and share a practical structure we know works and has been battle-tested firsthand at our own school sites and across schools we support throughout the United States at every level, from preK through middle school, high school, alternative education programs, and even non-brick-and-mortar virtual schools.

Over the years of implementing behavior academies across a variety of age levels and settings, we have simplified the approach of delivering behavior interventions—the *how* is what we describe next as the *behavior academy structure*. This structure is the *vehicle* to design and deliver effective behavior academies (behavior interventions), and it has three core components: (1) the initial session, (2) the ongoing sessions, and (3) the exit session (see figure 3.1).

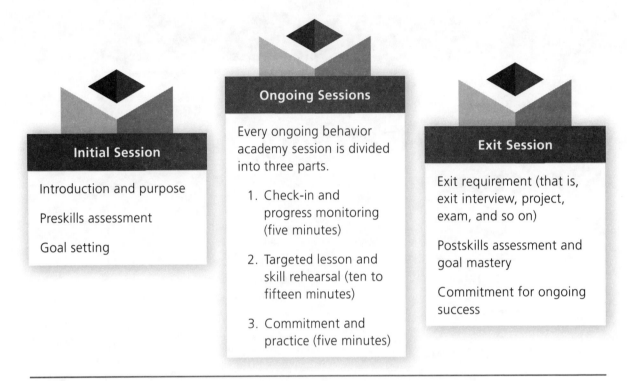

Initial Session

Introduction and purpose

Preskills assessment

Goal setting

Ongoing Sessions

Every ongoing behavior academy session is divided into three parts.

1. Check-in and progress monitoring (five minutes)

2. Targeted lesson and skill rehearsal (ten to fifteen minutes)

3. Commitment and practice (five minutes)

Exit Session

Exit requirement (that is, exit interview, project, exam, and so on)

Postskills assessment and goal mastery

Commitment for ongoing success

FIGURE 3.1: Three core components of the behavior academy structure.

In determining these three components, our number one priority is to ensure the thinking and practicality of this design makes sense to the educators delivering our behavior academy interventions. A student must know the purpose and goal they are working toward, the ongoing sessions must provide additional tools for their inner toolkit to practice and generalize these newly learned skills to reach their goals, and lastly, students need to demonstrate mastery and the ability to apply the learning independently to help them in school and life before we begin to consider removing these additional supports. That is what the structure illustrated in figure 3.1 captures.

We also want to note this behavior academy structure provides the most formalized level of behavior academy implementation for either individual or small groups of students based on needs. Specifically, this structure requires the ongoing consistent application aligned with behavior academy goals that require ongoing progress monitoring of effectiveness in a structured fashion. To consider the behavior academy as an evidence-based intervention, all three of the components featured in this chapter need to be in place with fidelity.

At the end of this chapter, we provide some informal behavior academy application suggestions. The differences in implementation of such informal application of behavior academies lie in the frequency of behavior academy delivery (can be as needed or decided by the person delivering the content), size of group (there is no restriction on group size), and presence (or nonpresence) of a formal goal setting or ongoing progress-monitoring component. In these cases, educators (or parents or guardians) use the tools from behavior academies as needed, such as classroom prevention used situationally if teachers wish to target specific skills through prevention, schoolwide prevention with a focus skill each week, or even at home where parents or guardians can use the replacement behaviors to target and teach their own child new life skills.

However, the following sections in this chapter define each of the three core components of the most formalized delivery of behavior academies, the behavior academy structure, and what they each entail. We also provide examples of these three core components using the Hands-Off Behavior Academy as a model. Again, this is the most formalized way of delivering behavior academies, and it is what we recommend for students who have demonstrated an ongoing need for additional time and support with targeted life skills.

Initial Session

The *initial session* core component is designed to help introduce students to the behavior academy design and purpose. This is the opportunity for the educator to assess directly from the student or students their current level of mastery of the eight life skills being targeted in the academy, any knowledge related to the behavior academy, and goal setting. The educator providing the academy can and should also consider any previous information regarding why the student is a candidate for this academy as part of this initial session. For example, a student may have had repeated write-ups for this behavior, a staff member might have completed a prereferral or support form request, a student might have self-referred, or an existing behavior intervention team on campus may have deemed the academy necessary based on student data and observations (or the student was a good match for the academy). Regardless of entrance criteria, the person delivering the academy should have access to prior knowledge to support goal setting and delivery of the academy. It is important for the educator delivering the behavior academy to know the purpose and why for the behavior academy and equally important for the students receiving the behavior academy to know as well.

We have witnessed, all too often, educators struggling to explain the purpose of certain behavior interventions they are delivering or what they are helping students accomplish (intended outcomes), so it's important to ensure this understanding is in place intentionally, right from the initial session of the behavior academy (see figure 3.2, page 28).

To summarize, the behavior academy structure initial session core component should be inclusive of the following.

- ▸ **Introduction and purpose:** Students need to know why they are in the behavior academy and its purpose. It is also important for the person delivering the academy to lean in from a place of empathy, understanding, and support from the beginning.

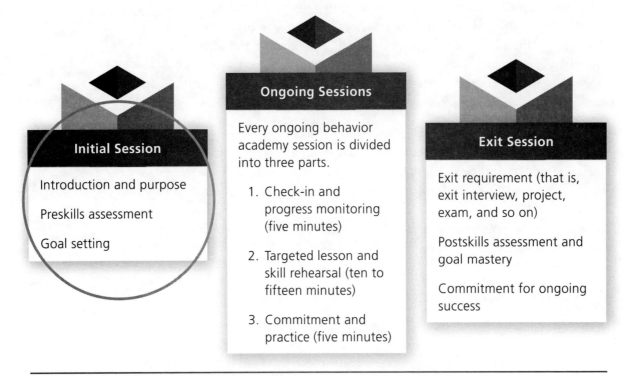

FIGURE 3.2: The initial session of the behavior academy structure.

> ▶ **Preskills assessment:** Students were placed in the academy based on specific entrance criteria, such as those listed at the start of this section. Regardless of the specifics, the educator providing the academy needs to have a clear idea of what life skills the student or students in the academy need support with.
>
> We provide the following three methods of preskills assessment you might draw from:
>
> a. The first method utilizes preexisting information regarding student behavior that is the catalyst for needing the academy in the first place. We utilize a behavior academy rubric (lead version) to capture this information, which will be explained in depth later in this chapter.
>
> b. The second method is interviewing the student or students or assessing their current knowledge of the eight targeted life skills before beginning the academy's ongoing sessions. We utilize a student version of the behavior academy rubric to gauge the student's level of understanding and application of the eight targeted life skills, and/or we provide the student with the eight scenarios from the corresponding behavior academy rehearsal cards (explained in detail in the ongoing session section) and ask them to explain how they would respond to each. This gives us a good idea of what replacement behaviors are their current go-tos or if they know the replacement behaviors but struggle to utilize them in certain situations.

c. The third method is to use a combination of both preceding methods to decide the baseline. In the next section, we provide some tools we have utilized to help.

▶ **Goal setting:** Goals (whether one goal or more than one) need to be aligned with the exit criterion of the academy, and students need to understand them. This provides students with a target and will be a key part of their progress monitoring during ongoing sessions. We have too often seen behavior interventions provided with no clear goal or outcome in mind. It is equally important for both the educator and the student to understand and know their goals. We also want to emphasize the academy goals need to be realistic, attainable, and aligned with the academy focus. We recommend monitoring no more than one to two goals consistently at a time. We have seen some educators set unrealistic goals or expectations for students, which creates an inaccurate impression the academy is ineffective. For example, we have seen students in a Hands-Off Academy meet their goal of zero hands-on incidents, yet are not celebrated for meeting their goal and are told how poorly they were behaving because they kept blurting out in class or wouldn't stay seated in the cafeteria. Remember, the student's goals are connected to the specific criterion of the academy; in this case, zero hands-on incidents.

In the following sections, we model the introduction and purpose, preskills assessment, and goal setting of the initial session using our Hands-Off Academy as an example to guide your thinking about this structure and format. Remember, this initial session is critical for a strong start and calibration for the work ahead. Trust and rapport building will be essential in this initial session and throughout the behavior academy delivery.

Initial Session: Introduction and Purpose

Introduction and purpose are designed to ensure students know *why* they are in the behavior academy and the purpose of the academy. It also allows students to have a voice in their learning and growth. We recommend the educator delivering the academy have some background knowledge and context on the students they are delivering the academy for. If the educator is prepared and ready to go with a plan for this initial session, it should take no more than twenty-five minutes to provide this level of targeted support. We have provided the following short introduction and purpose script to help guide the initial session meeting.

Welcome to the Hands-Off Behavior Academy. This behavior academy is designed to help you respond appropriately when you are upset or mad at a person or situation. I know this has been an area you have been struggling with recently, and that is why I am here to help you learn new life skills to use when you find yourself in difficult situations. We will set your goals together and work together to achieve them. I need your help in order to help you learn and practice these skills.

Our strongest suggestion in this stage is to humanize yourself. Explain to the students that no one is perfect at mastering all life skills, and you are there to help them develop more tools for their inner toolkit. It is important the students know they have caring adults who are not going to give up on them and will support them throughout this learning journey together.

Please do not print this script and read it verbatim to students; that would break rapport and come across as disingenuous. Instead, note the essence of this script— humanizing the experience; "We are working on building these skills together," and "I am here to support you toward meeting your goal." This is a disarming experience for students who feel like they are in trouble and this is their punishment. Remember, the process of establishing trust and rapport starts in this initial session, which is also why this initial session should take place in a safe and private setting. This may be in an office, classroom, or outside. It is wherever the students and educators providing the academy feel most comfortable.

Initial Session: Preskills Assessment

The *preskills assessment* is a necessary step in expanding the purpose in the introduction script. This also provides the basis for you as the person delivering the behavior academy as well as for the students participating in it. For example, if a student entered this behavior academy based on incidents of hands-on behavior, it is important to utilize that information along with the life skills you are targeting through this additional time and support to see a reduction of hands-on behavior. When we say preskills assessment, all we are saying is we (the adults) and the students need to be on the same page about where the students are with these life skills prior to the ongoing sessions of the behavior academy (a baseline, per se). The entire point is that students in the academy exit the academy with newly learned, productive life skills. So, in the case of a Hands-Off Academy, a successful implementation would result in included students no longer using their hands-on behavior to resolve conflict.

Let us first say we recognize there are several methods of conducting preskills assessments (to get a baseline). We work with schools that have commonly used behavior screeners already in place, such as DESSA, Panorama, SAEBRS, SDQ, SELweb, and so on. If you are in such a district, and these methods are working for you, use what you currently have in place for this core component to assess baseline. Other schools may have an effective behavior intervention team whose members regularly meet to identify and match students based on repeated behavior data points and perception data. These are also good measures of a preassessment of skills (the baseline). Here, we simply want to provide some additional tools and suggestions on how to assess preskills for schools that don't currently have methods in place at the beginning of a behavior academy.

Figure 3.3 shows a sample Hands-Off Academy rubric lead version as well as a student version preskills rubric to illustrate this process. (See page 166 for a reproducible version of this figure, useable with any behavior academy.) To begin, the Hands-Off Academy rubric lead version is aligned with the eight life skills that will be targeted throughout this academy.

Targeted Life Skills	Minimal to No Mastery	Emergent Mastery	Internalized Mastery	Pre-Academy Score	Post-Academy Score

Hands-Off Behavior Academy Rubric: Lead Version

Behavior Academy Lead Name: *JH*

Student in the Academy: *Fahn*

Targeted Life Skills	Minimal to No Mastery Student inconsistently demonstrates or does not demonstrate (0)	Emergent Mastery Student demonstrates with prompt or cue (1)	Internalized Mastery Student independently demonstrates (2)	Pre-Academy Score Date: *10-2-23*	Post-Academy Score Date: _____
Skill: Self-reflection				*0*	
Skill: Conflict resolution				*0*	
Skill: Impulse control				*0*	
Skill: Identifying emotional triggers				*0*	
Skill: Self-regulation				*0*	
Skill: Accountability				*0*	
Skill: Help seeking				*1*	
Skill: Communication (verbal and nonverbal)				*1*	
Rubric mastery:	Rubric assessment mastery is 13–16 range by the end of the behavior academy. Rubric assessment mastery Met or Not Met = *Not Met (Pre-Academy Total = 2)*				
Notes and observations: *Fahn has repeated office referrals for hands-on behavior (average 4 in a 2-week period). Fahn was also matched to the Hands-Off Academy based on the behavior intervention team's recommendation.*				Pre-Academy Total = *2*	Post-Academy Total = ____

FIGURE 3.3: Hands-Off Behavior Academy rubric—Lead version.

As you can see in figure 3.3, the targeted eight life skills for Hands-Off Behavior Academy are listed in the first column on the left (self-reflection, conflict resolution, and so on). Also, notice the rubric of Minimal to No Mastery (0), Emergent Mastery (1), and Internalized Mastery (2) because our ultimate outcome is for students to turn these newly learned life skills into new productive habits (internalized mastery) and utilize them when in challenging situations. In reality, the highest level of outcome we can reach is for the students to independently use these newly learned skills whether we are there to help them or not (internalized level). Lastly, there are Pre-Academy and Post-Academy Scores as evidence of growth in the columns on the right. So, the educator providing the behavior academy can complete the lead rubric prior (based on previous knowledge and input from stakeholders, existing screener data, and so on), complete it during the initial conversation with the student, or both. For example, figure 3.3 shows a rubric completed for a student named Fahn, who was matched to the behavior academy by the existing behavior intervention team. The lead for this

Student Name: *Fahn*		
Hands-Off Academy Skills	Define in your own words what each skill means. If you do not know, please write "I don't know."	*If you know what the skill means, how often would you say you utilize this skill instead of using hands-on behavior when you are upset or angry? **Scale:** 1 = Never 2 = Rarely 3 = Sometimes 4 = Often 5 = Always
Skill: Self-reflection	*I don't know.*	Circle ① 2 3 4 5
Skill: Conflict resolution	*I don't know.*	Circle ① 2 3 4 5
Skill: Impulse control	*I don't know.*	Circle ① 2 3 4 5
Skill: Identifying emotional triggers	*I don't know.*	Circle ① 2 3 4 5
Skill: Self-regulation	*I don't know.*	Circle ① 2 3 4 5
Skill: Accountability	*I don't know.*	Circle ① 2 3 4 5
Skill: Help seeking	*When I ask the teacher for help when someone is making me mad*	Circle 1 ② 3 4 5
Skill: Communication (verbal and nonverbal)	*I don't know.*	Circle 1 ② 3 4 5
Rubric mastery:	Rubric assessment mastery is 32 or above range (80% or higher) by the end of the behavior academy. Rubric assessment mastery Met or Not Met = *Not Met* *(Pre-Academy Total = 10)*	

Notes and observations: *Student responded to each item.*	**Pre-Academy** Total = _10_	**Post-Academy** Total = ____

FIGURE 3.4: Hands-Off Behavior Academy rubric—Student version.

academy knew, based on previous data and the recommendation from the behavior intervention team, that Fahn was struggling to demonstrate the eight targeted life skills as indicated by the Pre-Academy Score of 2. This was further confirmed when the lead asked Fahn a series of questions using the student version of this rubric depicted in figure 3.4. (See page 167 for a reproducible version of this figure usable with any behavior academy.)

As mentioned, the student version of the rubric helped the lead see for herself Fahn's areas of need. In the Hands-Off Behavior Academy Rubric—Student Version, you will find the same eight targeted life skills listed; however, students are asked—with the guidance of the lead delivering the behavior academy—to self-reflect on their current knowledge and frequency of using these eight targeted life skills, as depicted in figure 3.4. Students are asked to define and reflect on their use of the eight targeted life skills using a frequency scale of 1 = Never, 2 = Rarely, 3 = Sometimes, 4 = Often, 5 = Always. Note you can use the student version of the rubric at the beginning and end of the academy.

Both preskills assessment tools will aid the person delivering the behavior academy to gather and affirm baseline data and to prioritize skills to teach first. For example, *self-reflection* may be the first targeted life skill listed on the behavior rehearsal card, but you identify *self-regulation* being the highest need skill to start with. Another consideration, as mentioned prior, to help gather baseline data is to provide students in the academy with the scenarios from the behavior rehearsal cards that go along with each academy and discern how they respond. This is further explained in the Ongoing Sessions section (page 34), but there are eight scenarios that go along with the eight targeted life skills in each academy. You can provide the students with the scenarios and note how they respond at the beginning of an academy, then provide all eight scenarios again at the end of the academy to see how they apply their newly learned targeted life skills in their responses. There is no wrong way of doing this, but the important thing is that we know where the students are with these skills at the beginning and end of the academy. To measure student progress, you'll need this baseline information, which will then be used to set realistic goals. At a minimum, we say to use a preassessment such as the rubric we provided to gather baseline. However, we do know some educators who use the rubrics we provided to help progress monitor at least twice a month beyond just the preassessment. That is a personal preference based on the person delivering the behavior academy.

This brings us to the last core component in the initial session, goal setting.

Initial Session: Goal Setting

During the initial session component of goal setting, it is essential to create realistic goals and ensure the student understands the goals being set. For example, a student may have entered a Hands-Off Academy due to having three or four office discipline referrals for hands-on behavior over a two-week period, or staff noticed the student struggling to utilize appropriate skills when angry at other students or situations. The goal (or goals) set needs to reflect how we change this narrative that placed the students in the behavior academy to begin with. For example, here we provide two samples of Hands-Off Academy goals.

▶ **Example Hands-Off Academy goal 1:** *I will have zero office discipline referrals for hands-on behavior each week for a period of six to eight weeks (baseline: average of three or four hands-on behavior office discipline referrals in a two-week period).*

> ▸ **Example Hands-Off Academy goal 2:** *I will consistently use my learned skills from Hands-Off Academy when I am angry or perceive a situation as unfair instead of resorting to hands-on behaviors for a period of six to eight weeks. This will be measured by consistently using newly learned skills throughout the school day and having a post-behavior academy score of 13 or higher (baseline: inconsistently utilizing appropriate skills based on teacher and administrator observations and pre-academy rubric [lead version] total score of 2).*

It is recommended each behavior academy have one or two goals at maximum. This ensures the targeted focus. Our focus in a Hands-Off Academy is that the students discontinue having hands-on incidents; therefore, this is what the goal should be based on for all students in the Hands-Off Academy. The second goal example provided is based on a pre-academy rubric (lead version) total score. Both goals are aligned with the purpose of the behavior academy at hand. It makes sense: we want those who are in the academy to stop having hands-on incidents and to use their newly learned targeted life skills (replacement behaviors) instead.

To reemphasize, the main point of the goal-setting component in the initial session is to ensure the goal is aligned with behaviors that placed students in this academy in the first place and to provide a target for students so they know what is required to exit this academy. For this specific Hands-Off Academy example, students' goals should be aligned with zero incidents of hands-on behavior and teacher and administrator perception ratings showing each student in the academy is generalizing the newly learned skills. Educators can adjust these goals based on the intended outcomes for the behavior academies being delivered, but we want to give a concrete example of what should be reflected through your goals in alignment with the purpose of the academy.

Figure 3.5 provides an example weekly attendance- and goal-monitoring log as a tool highlighting Fahn as an example of a student who was in eight weeks (about two months) of a Hands-Off Academy. (See page 168 for a blank reproducible version of this figure.)

To summarize, in this initial session core component of the behavior academy structure, students and the educators providing the behavior academy need to know why they are in the academy and have a clear sense of what their outcomes of the academy are. Next, we explain the structure of the ongoing session's core components.

Ongoing Sessions

The *ongoing sessions* core component is designed to provide educators with a practical method of delivering behavior academies; this is your *how to* for each ongoing behavior academy session. This section outlines the simple yet effective design of what happens during each ongoing session of a behavior academy. Although the number of sessions for an academy, the session frequency, and the session length can vary based on need, we recommend targeting eight once-per-week ongoing sessions that last about twenty-five minutes or less per session. Remember, each behavior academy focuses on at least

	Attendance		Goal	
	Present	**Not Present**	**Met**	**Not Met**
Week 1	☑	☐	☑	☐
Week 2	☐	☑	☐	☑
Week 3	☑	☐	☑	☐
Week 4	☑	☐	☑	☐
Week 5	☑	☐	☑	☐
Week 6	☑	☐	☑	☐
Week 7	☑	☐	☑	☐
Week 8	☑	☐	☑	☐

Student name: *Fahn*

Behavior academy goal (or goals):

1. *I will have zero office discipline referrals for hands-on behavior each week for a period of six to eight weeks.*

FIGURE 3.5: Hands-Off Academy attendance- and goal-monitoring log.

eight targeted life skills, so each session focuses on the teaching and practice of these targeted life skills and their corresponding replacement behaviors. Once you conduct a few behavior academy ongoing sessions, you'll see how the structure repeats itself and becomes very easy to do. It also provides an emotionally safe and predictable structure for students to learn and practice their newly learned targeted life skills.

Every behavior academy ongoing session is organized into these three parts: (1) check-in and progress monitoring (five minutes), (2) targeted lesson and skill rehearsal (ten to fifteen minutes), (3) commitment and practice (five minutes). We have purposely designed these ongoing sessions to be brief in duration due to the attention span of students. We also find, based on our experiences implementing behavior academy ongoing sessions, the more intentional and targeted they are, the better. Simply put, focusing on one targeted life skill at a time is most effective. We also realize educators have limited time, so we want to ensure they can use their time with the students sensibly and efficiently. It is essential that each of these parts is represented during each session, which should be no more than twenty-five minutes long.

As you can see in figure 3.6 (page 36), this is the largest section of the entire behavior academy structure, and for good reason. Each ongoing session is designed to ensure educators are helping students: (1) monitor their success toward the behavior academy goals and navigate through possible setbacks and barriers to success, (2) learn and rehearse new targeted life skills and replacement behaviors, and (3) commit to ongoing application of these newly learned targeted life skills (develop productive habits).

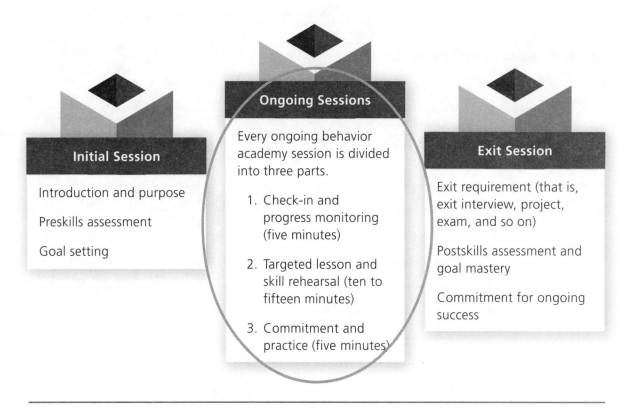

FIGURE 3.6: The ongoing sessions of the behavior academy structure.

To summarize, the behavior academy structure ongoing sessions core component should be inclusive of the following.

1. **Check-in and progress monitoring (five minutes):** Students need to learn how to self-monitor their behavior academy goals in each ongoing session. They also need to learn how to work through setbacks and identify and avoid barriers to their success.

2. **Targeted lesson and skill rehearsal (ten to fifteen minutes):** Students need to be taught the definition of the targeted life skill and provided with one or two replacement behaviors to help them demonstrate that life skill. Students also need to receive opportunities to practice the targeted life skills and replacement behaviors, and continue to rehearse previously learned life skills.

3. **Commitment and practice (five minutes):** Students need support in making a commitment to practice newly learned skills and generalize them in less-structured settings after each ongoing session (developing productive habits).

To ensure consistency during each ongoing behavior academy session, we provide a behavior academy ongoing sessions lesson plan template for reference (see figure 3.7). (See page 169 for a reproducible version of this figure.) Specifically, this template is designed to help educators ensure fidelity in what is being delivered during each ongoing session: (1) check-in and progress monitoring, (2) targeted lesson and skill rehearsal, and (3) commitment and practice. After delivering a few behavior academy ongoing sessions using this lesson plan template as a guide, educators often find

1. Check-in and progress monitoring (five minutes)

Have students complete their self-monitoring form goal check-in with your supervision and guidance. Celebrate wins, and be prepared to help them navigate setbacks or barriers to success. Revisit previously learned session targeted skill and replacement behaviors: What skill and replacement behaviors did we learn during the last session?

2. Targeted lesson and skill rehearsal (ten to fifteen minutes)

Review the behavior rehearsal card skill focus definition and replacement behaviors.

Today's targeted life skill focuses of the session:	Skill definition in students' words after looking it up or discussing the definition with the students:
	What are some replacement behaviors to help demonstrate the targeted life skill focus (also provide one or two replacement behaviors)?

Behavior Rehearsal Card Session Scenario

Have students:

- Review the behavior rehearsal card scenario
- Say the skill focus and read the scenario
- Share the right way and wrong way to respond to the scenario
- Rehearse one or two of the taught replacement behaviors they can use to demonstrate the right way to respond if they were in that scenario

Student-Developed Scenario and Application

Help students:

- Come up with another similar scenario related to the focus area they may have experienced (if time permits)
- Develop the right way and wrong way to respond
- Rehearse one or two of the taught replacement behaviors they can use to demonstrate the right way to respond if they were in that scenario

3. Commitment and practice (five minutes)

Practice throughout the week: help the student or students identify at least one targeted life skill (replacement behavior) to work on this week, and complete a written and/or verbal commitment to practice that identified life skill (replacement behavior).

FIGURE 3.7: Behavior academy ongoing sessions lesson plan template.

themselves not needing this template because the process becomes internalized for the person delivering it. Please pause and take a moment to review the behavior academy ongoing sessions lesson plan template.

Ongoing Sessions: Check-In and Progress Monitoring

Picture this: students are now in a behavior academy ongoing session, and the educator is following the lesson plan template depicted in figure 3.7 (page 37), but what are the students doing to log their learning through these three parts just described? We have included such a tool—a behavior academy student progress-monitoring document—with versions to support both older and younger students (figure 3.8 and figure 3.9, page 40). (See page 170 and page 172 for reproducible versions of these figures.)

Student name: _____	Date: _____

1 CHECK-IN AND PROGRESS MONITORING	
Behavior academy goal:	Circle one: Met Partially Met Not Met
Behavior academy goal:	Circle one: Met Partially Met Not Met

What worked for you toward attaining your weekly goals?

What didn't work for you toward attaining your weekly goals?

Review: What was our skill focus last session? Review: What replacement behaviors did you learn to help you demonstrate this skill focus?	Were you able to apply the learned replacement behaviors successfully in any scenarios this past week? Explain.

2 TARGETED LESSON AND SKILL REHEARSAL

Today's skill focus of the session:	Skill definition:
	Replacement behaviors to help demonstrate the skill focus:

Behavior rehearsal card session scenario:	**Student-developed scenario and application:**
What is the skill focus?	What is another scenario about this skill focus you have experienced?
What is the right way to respond?	What is the right way to respond?
What is the wrong way to respond?	What is the wrong way to respond?
What is one replacement behavior that can help with the right way for this scenario?	What is one replacement behavior that can help with the right way for this scenario?

3 COMMITMENT AND PRACTICE

Practice throughout the week:

I _____ will work on _____ this week in order to meet my behavior goal (or goals).

Student signature: _____

FIGURE 3.8: Behavior academy student progress-monitoring form—Older students.

Student name: _____   **Date:** _____

How did I do this week? Circle one:

☺   😐   ☹

Draw or explain why you circled the face you did.

Draw or write one thing you learned about the last time we met.

Today's new skill is _____.
Draw or write what this skill looks like or sounds like.

Draw or write one thing you can do to show this new skill.

New skill: What is the right way to respond?

New skill: What is the wrong way to respond?

I _____ will practice _____ this week.

Student signature: _____

FIGURE 3.9: Behavior academy student progress-monitoring form—Younger students.

These documents are fully aligned with the behavior academy ongoing sessions lesson plan template: (1) check-in and progress monitoring, (2) targeted lesson and skill rehearsal, and (3) commitment and practice. While the educator is facilitating each item from the lesson plan template, the students have a process (graphic organizer) to log their learning. For example, you can staple the progress-monitoring forms in a manila folder during each session. This way, students can also see their progress and all their skills and replacement behaviors learned over time. It is up to the educators delivering the academy to decide the method they prefer, but we have found keeping to a consistent structure each ongoing session helps tremendously. Please pause and reflect on the behavior academy student progress-monitoring form examples and how they correspond with the ongoing behavior academy lesson plan template just described.

Utilizing the ongoing lesson plan template ensures each session begins with a straightforward progress-monitoring structure with a consistent check-in, new targeted skill focus (replacement behaviors taught and rehearsed), and ends with another straightforward prompt for commitment and practice. However, the targeted lesson and skill rehearsal, utilizing what we refer to as *behavior rehearsal cards*, will require a more detailed explanation than what is offered on the lesson plan template.

Ongoing Sessions: Targeted Lesson and Skill Rehearsal

So now you have learned what it takes to plan and organize for the initial behavior academy session. Ideally, this would mean you have held your initial session with students. You and the students are clear about the baseline and the goals of the academy, but now what? What do we do when the students are in front of us, ready for the delivery of the first targeted lesson? At this point, you need a quick and proven way to teach and rehearse the identified targeted life skills and corresponding replacement behaviors during the targeted lesson and skill rehearsal of the behavior academy session. *Behavior rehearsal cards* are a fast, easy way to do it. These cards capture all the content necessary to help an educator quickly and efficiently work with students on at least one targeted life skill and teach and practice two replacement behaviors per week. Think of it as a behavior intervention on a card because each card holds the information needed to conduct a behavior academy ongoing session. Let us explain the thinking behind its design.

Each behavior academy has a set of eight behavior rehearsal cards (eight targeted life skills—one on each behavior rehearsal card). Each behavior rehearsal card includes the targeted life skill and definition, two possible replacement behaviors to help students practice and generalize the targeted life skill, a rehearsal and application scenario, and an opportunity for the students to create their own scenario for additional practice. Figure 3.10 (page 42) is an example of a behavior rehearsal card from Hands-Off Academy with the targeted skill of self-reflection to illustrate our thinking.

Front of Behavior Rehearsal Card	Back of Behavior Rehearsal Card

Targeted life skill: **SELF-REFLECTION**

Hands-Off Academy

Definition: The ability to look inward to understand how your thoughts, feelings, and behaviors impact your overall behavior and personal growth

Replacement behaviors:

Three Rs (<u>r</u>ewind, <u>r</u>eplay, <u>r</u>edo)—Imagine the incident you experienced as a short video you can play in your head. Imagine having the ability to rewind, replay, and redo as many times as you need. Imagine where you were, where the other person was (or people were), what you said or did, what they said or did, how it made you feel, and how you responded.

Now, use the 3Rs. **R**ewind the incident, and **r**eplay it in your head or talk through it out loud. Then, **r**edo the part of the incident where things went wrong. Think about one or two ways you would change (redo) your response in the future, such as taking back your reaction and use of hands-on behavior.

Voice memo to self—Imagine yourself using a voice memo app on your phone or device. A voice memo is usually a short recording of yourself speaking to yourself in a way that allows you to express your feelings and self-reflect in a safe place. Act like you are recording a short voice memo (message) to yourself about the incident and what you learned from it. Allow yourself to replay scenes from this incident and the challenges you faced. Pay close attention to how you felt in these moments. What emotions did you experience? How did your body feel? Speak each thought as it comes, focusing on honesty and openness. As you finish, imagine wrapping up your thoughts like the end of a story. Last, picture yourself in the future, listening back to your voice memo. What would you tell yourself that may help you in the future? Remember, you are not actually recording this on a device but using this as an exercise to self-reflect.

Rehearsal and application scenario:

Abel and Jared were involved in a fight during a football game disagreement. While Jared took some time to reflect on the fight and what he could have done instead to solve the problem, Abel did not think twice about his role in the fight.

Wrong way to respond? Right way to respond?

Student-created scenario:

Wrong way to respond? Right way to respond?

FIGURE 3.10: Hands-Off Academy behavior rehearsal card example.

The example of the behavior rehearsal card in figure 3.10 is only one of eight targeted life skills that make up our Hands-Off Academy. Here, we provide an example of one behavior rehearsal card first (self-reflection) to model the thinking before providing additional rehearsal cards in chapter 4 (page 57). As you can see in this behavior rehearsal card example, there are two replacement behaviors listed (three Rs and voice memo to self). This is an important feature because we not only want students to learn what the new targeted life skill is, we also need easy, practical ways to demonstrate the targeted life skill they are learning during each session.

We define *replacement behaviors* as a way to help students think about the unproductive behavior they want to replace and how to do it effectively. We want students to have an inner toolkit of replacement behaviors they can instinctively pull from to demonstrate each targeted life skill.

More specifically, the replacement behaviors on the behavior rehearsal cards were developed using the psychology behind visualization and mental imagery to teach and develop new productive habits. Mental imagery is involved in many everyday cognitive functions and also plays a special role in representing our past and future experiences, a role that is believed to facilitate adaptive decision-making, planning, and self-regulatory behavior. Importantly, the ability for mental imagery to emulate real-life experience can powerfully impact emotion and motivation (Ji, Kavanagh, Holmes, MacLeod, & Di Simplicio, 2019). Mental imagery, when used effectively, can provide concrete visualization for abstract concepts.

Elite athletes have been using visualization and mental imagery exercises for decades. Repeatedly visualizing activities (mental rehearsals) such as running a race or throwing a pass hundreds of times strengthens the same neural pathways in the brain as actually doing the activity, so when they experience these activities in real life, it is not unfamiliar and feels as though they have experienced it before. We want to create similar experiences for students in ways that go beyond traditional methods of using worksheets, which train the wrong part of the brain.

You can see in our example behavior rehearsal card that to improve the targeted life skill of self-reflection, students can utilize what we refer to as the *three Rs* and *voice memo to self* as two ways to do so (two replacement behaviors using imagery to help students demonstrate self-reflection). If you intend to use our behavior rehearsal cards as designed during the ongoing sessions, specifically teaching the replacement behaviors using imagery, we recommend using a mini exercise prior to introducing the imagery-based replacement behaviors for the first time. For example, an educator can do a couple of things to get the student in the mind frame of using imagery by:

▸ Defining what imagery means and providing some samples

▸ Having students engage in an imagery exercise thinking about their favorite food or ice cream; for example, have them imagine getting ready to eat it, identifying with their senses what they taste, see, feel, and so on.

As the educator working with students, you can provide additional or different replacement behaviors and strategies beyond those recommended in this book. Here, we provide a targeted life skill and two possible replacement behaviors using imagery to get you started for each ongoing session. Although we recommend at least one ongoing session per week, it does not mean you cannot increase the frequency of your sessions. For example, some students may need help twice a week to focus on that one targeted life skill and corresponding replacement behaviors, and some students may demonstrate learning and application faster than others, while other students may need additional practice with these skills. We recommend increasing frequency over duration if a student needs more. We find that students are more productive in two twenty-five-minute sessions than if the duration of one session is increased from twenty-five to fifty minutes. Here, we focus on not just giving you a place to begin but most importantly, a *process* to utilize.

We would also like to note that although we prefer using our behavior rehearsal cards during these ongoing sessions due to practicality and efficiency purposes, this doesn't mean educators cannot add additional tools, resources, curricula, and multiple modalities as they are teaching new targeted life skills and corresponding replacement behaviors. The point, however, remains the same: students need to receive, at minimum, at least one or two replacement behaviors during each session to help demonstrate the targeted skill focus of the ongoing session. For example, many districts have adopted curricula such as Second Step, Ripple Effects, and so on that can be used during the targeted lesson skill delivery and teaching session of an academy. Use what you have to supplement the teaching, and if you want or need more resources to pull from, just add it specifically to the core component targeted lesson and skill rehearsal (ten to fifteen minutes) of the ongoing sessions. Ultimately, we want you to have practical tools regardless of the level of resources available to you.

The important thing to remember when supplementing is the targetedness that sometimes sequenced ready-made curricula may not capture. For example, we would not delay the teaching of empathy to a student in November because the scope and sequence of a behavior curriculum says that February is empathy month. We teach empathy when that is a targeted skill a student needs to work on now.

Ongoing Sessions: Commitment and Practice

At the end of each ongoing session, typically the last five minutes of the session, it is important to help the student commit to practicing (continuing to rehearse) these newly learned replacement behaviors either in written or verbal format. We encourage the behavior academy lead to help ensure students are clear on what they are working on. And remember, we provided student self-monitoring forms during these ongoing sessions that include a section at the end for commitment and practice before the next session.

An additional recommendation for the person providing the behavior academy ongoing session is to also inform other stakeholders on what targeted life skill and corresponding replacement behaviors students are practicing so these stakeholders (teachers, administrators, and even parents and guardians) can help support the practice of these skills when the students are in their presence over the course of a typical day. This way, all stakeholders can reinforce and/or remind the student to use their newly learned replacement behaviors if they see the student in a challenging situation and celebrate the wins with the student when they see the student demonstrating their prosocial behaviors.

Another suggestion is to teach students and stakeholders a behavior academy code word or nonverbal signal such as the code word *activate* or a hand signal reminding students to activate the replacement behaviors they have been learning in the behavior academy ongoing sessions. For example, a teacher may notice a student who is in the Hands-Off Academy start to appear frustrated and angry, and the teacher may show the reminder signal to the student or verbally remind the student to activate newly learned skills. This may be a good buffer for students as they are learning how to generalize the newly learned skills.

To summarize, each behavior academy ongoing session should include (1) check-in and progress monitoring (five minutes), (2) targeted lesson and skill rehearsal (ten to fifteen minutes), and (3) commitment and practice (five minutes). We have provided tools and guidance on what needs to take place during each session and how to get yourself and the students organized for each ongoing behavior academy session; we now move to what the exit session entails.

Exit Session

The last core component of the behavior academy structure is the exit session (see figure 3.11). When students consistently demonstrate mastery of their newly learned targeted life skills and have met the behavior academy exit criteria by consistently meeting their goals, this exit session is an opportunity for students to apply their learned skills through a variety of methods and commit for ongoing success.

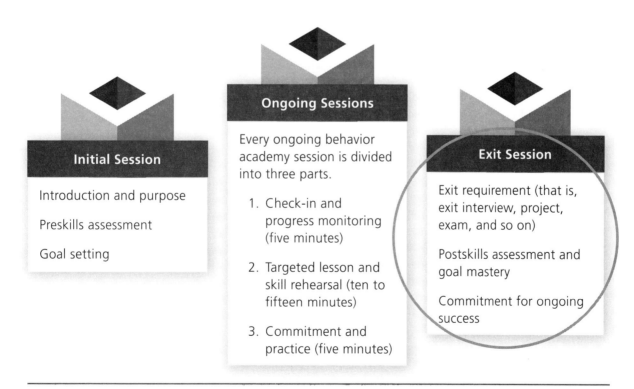

FIGURE 3.11: The exit session of the behavior academy structure.

To outline, the exit session should be inclusive of the following.

▸ **Exit requirement (that is, exit interview, project, exam, and so on):** Students are required to demonstrate evidence of mastery and application of the skills aligned with the behavior academy.

▸ **Postskills assessment:** Skills aligned with the behavior academy are assessed based on exit criteria and goals met. Postskills assessment rubrics are utilized (adult and student versions).

▸ **Commitment for ongoing success:** Students are required to make a commitment to continue using the learned skills.

Exit Session: Exit Requirement

The *exit requirement* during this session is designed to help culminate the behavior academy experience with evidence of mastery and application. There are a variety of ways you may choose to do this, but we have provided a list of possible exit requirement options as a reference (see figure 3.12). We like providing students with the opportunity to not only celebrate their success but also apply their learning to help themselves or other students in the future.

Directions: Provided is a list of options to help you decide what exit requirements you would like to implement.

- Give examples of mastery in an exam format.
- Have students respond to the eight scenarios from each of the eight behavior rehearsal cards from the corresponding behavior academy (oral or written format).
- Finish a writing prompt aligned with the newly learned behavior academy skills.
- Identify a problem in the school or community similar to the scenarios and create a resource to help.
- Construct a service-learning project to address the targeted behavior.
- Help design and teach a lesson about the behavior topic.
- Present to a younger group on the learned behavior skills.
- Give an exit interview (have a stakeholder sign off on the student's skill demonstration).
- Film a video demonstrating the appropriate ways to demonstrate each skill learned.
- Develop a how-to guide for others who need help with these skills.
- Collaborate on student-developed exit requirements.
- Engage in a self-reflection exercise.
- Offer student choice.

FIGURE 3.12: Exit requirement options.

*Visit **go.SolutionTree.com/behavior** for a free reproducible version of this figure.*

Exit Session: Postskills Assessment

The *postskills assessment* during the exit session is designed to capture the student's progress. This should be similar to what you did in the initial session when you assessed the preskills assessment (baseline) so you can compare the growth. As the lead of the behavior academy, you should have a good record of whether the student has demonstrated the necessary progress for exiting the academy on the postskills assessment prior to scheduling the exit session; nonetheless, this session will help you solidify the student's readiness to exit. We have provided a sample Hands-Off Academy rubric lead version (see figure 3.13), along with a Hands-Off Academy rubric student version (see figure 3.14, page 48) as a reference of tools to help with the postskills assessment. You can see they are the same as the preskills rubrics, so you can capture a consistent pre- and post-data analysis of effectiveness. Also, remember you can also provide the same eight scenarios on the behavior rehearsal cards and have the students provide descriptions of how they would respond. Pay close attention to observe if students are referencing the newly learned targeted life skills and replacement behaviors.

Hands-Off Behavior Academy Rubric: Lead Version					
Behavior Academy Lead Name: *JH*					
Student in the Academy: *Fahn*					
Targeted Life Skills	**Minimal to No Mastery** Student inconsistently demonstrates or does not demonstrate (0)	**Emergent Mastery** Student demonstrates with prompt or cue (1)	**Internalized Mastery** Student independently demonstrates (2)	**Pre-Academy Score** Date: *10-2-23*	**Post-Academy Score** Date: *11-20-23*
Skill: Self-reflection				*0*	*2*
Skill: Conflict resolution				*0*	*2*
Skill: Impulse control				*0*	*2*
Skill: Identifying emotional triggers				*0*	*2*
Skill: Self-regulation				*0*	*1*
Skill: Accountability				*0*	*1*
Skill: Help seeking				*1*	*2*
Skill: Communication (verbal and nonverbal)				*1*	*2*
Rubric mastery:	Rubric assessment mastery is 13–16 range by the end of the behavior academy. Rubric assessment mastery Met or Not Met = *Met (Post-Academy Total = 14)*				
Notes and observations *Fahn has had zero hands-on behavior referrals or incidents consistently in a six- to eight-week period.*				**Pre-Academy Total =** _2_	**Post-Academy Total =** _14_

FIGURE 3.13: Completed Hands-Off Behavior Academy rubric—Lead version.

Student Name: *Fahn*		
Hands-Off Academy Skills	Define in your own words what each skill means. If you do not know, please write "I don't know."	*If you know what the skill means, how often would you say you utilize this skill instead of using hands-on behavior when you are upset or angry? **Scale:** 1 = Never 2 = Rarely 3 = Sometimes 4 = Often 5 = Always
Skill: Self-reflection	*Think about what I am doing.*	Circle 1 2 3 ④ 5
Skill: Conflict resolution	*Apologize.*	Circle 1 2 ③ 4 5
Skill: Impulse control	*Remove myself from a situation that is making me mad.*	Circle 1 2 3 ④ 5
Skill: Identifying emotional triggers	*Pay attention to what my body is telling me.*	Circle 1 2 3 ④ 5
Skill: Self-regulation	*Take deep breaths.*	Circle 1 2 3 ④ 5
Skill: Accountability	*Own when I am wrong.*	Circle 1 2 3 ④ 5
Skill: Help seeking	*Ask a teacher for help.*	Circle 1 2 3 4 ⑤
Skill: Communication (verbal and nonverbal)	*Pay attention to what I am saying and what my body is also saying without words.*	Circle 1 2 3 ④ 5
Rubric mastery:	Rubric assessment mastery is 32 or above range (80% or higher) by the end of the behavior academy. Rubric assessment mastery Met or Not Met = *Met (Post-Academy Total = 32)*	

Notes and observations: *Student responded to each item.*	**Pre-Academy** Total = _10_	**Post-Academy** Total = _32_

FIGURE 3.14: Completed Hands-Off Behavior Academy rubric—Student version.

Commitment for Ongoing Success

The *commitment for ongoing success* is designed to help students make a commitment to continue applying these learned skills and provides a method for the lead of the behavior academy to help ensure the student maintains success into the future. In figure 3.15, we provide one example of our "write your new narrative" tool as a reference of what can be utilized in this exit session. (See page 173 for a reproducible version of this figure.) For younger students, you can also call this a "write your new story" individual contract.

Student name: _____ **Mentor or advisor name:** _____

Who am I?

_____

_____

_____

_____

What are some poor choices I have made in the past at school (my old narrative)?

_____

_____

_____

_____

What do I want to see for myself (my new narrative) when it comes to behavior and academics in school?

_____

_____

_____

_____

How do I plan on making this new narrative come true?

_____

_____

_____

_____

What help do I need to make this new narrative come true?

_____

_____

_____

_____

FIGURE 3.15: Write "your new narrative" individual contract.

continued →

Who will I reach out to and how often to help make this new narrative come true?

_____

_____

_____

_____

What are my short-term goals toward this new narrative?

_____

_____

_____

_____

What are my long-term goals toward this new narrative?

_____

_____

_____

_____

My work toward my new narrative will begin on: _____

Student signature of commitment to my new narrative: _____

Check-In Commitment Schedule

Date: _____   Check-in with: _____   Commitments: _____   Initials: ____

Date: _____   Check-in with: _____   Commitments: _____   Initials: ____

Date: _____   Check-in with: _____   Commitments: _____   Initials: ____

Date: _____   Check-in with: _____   Commitments: _____   Initials: ____

Date: _____   Check-in with: _____   Commitments: _____   Initials: ____

Date: _____   Check-in with: _____   Commitments: _____   Initials: ____

Date: _____   Check-in with: _____   Commitments: _____   Initials: ____

Date: _____   Check-in with: _____   Commitments: _____   Initials: ____

The majority of this chapter was designed to walk you through the most formalized fashion of a behavior academy's three core components: (1) the initial session, (2) the ongoing sessions, and (3) the exit session to ensure each is implemented with fidelity. Use the prompts and guiding questions in the behavior academy planning document featured in figure 3.16 to further help organize for a successful implementation. (See page 175 for a reproducible version of this figure.)

Who is leading the behavior academy: _____ **Start date:** _____	
Scheduled delivery date, time, and frequency: Once a week for twenty-five minutes: _____ Twice a week for twenty-five minutes: _____ Other: _____	
Behavior Academy name: ☐ Hands-Off Academy ☐ Check-In Check-Out Academy ☐ Civility Academy ☐ Organizational Skills Academy ☐ Social Skills Academy ☐ Upstander Academy ☐ Motivation Academy ☐ Emotional Regulation Academy Other: _____ Other: _____	Tactics to improve or maintain behavior academy structure:
Initial session planning components: introduction and purpose, preskills assessment, goal setting	
Introduction and purpose: What process will be utilized to introduce students to the purpose of the behavior academy?	
Preskills assessment: What targeted skills will be taught in this behavior academy? What method will be utilized to conduct a preskill assessment of these targeted skills in this behavior academy?	
Goal setting: What will the targeted goals be for this academy?	

FIGURE 3.16: Behavior academy planning document.   continued →

Ongoing sessions planning components: check-in and progress monitoring, targeted lesson and skill rehearsal, commitment and practice	
Check-in and progress monitoring: What process or tool will be utilized to check-in and progress monitor with the students during each behavior academy session? How will you help students process through setbacks or barriers to success?	
Targeted lesson and skill rehearsal: What method or curricula will be utilized to teach and practice the targeted life skills aligned with the behavior academy in each session? What replacement behaviors will you be teaching in each ongoing session to help the student with the targeted skill focus?	
Commitment and practice: What process or tool will be utilized during each session to help students identify their commitment and practice skills prior to the next session?	
Exit session planning components: exit requirement, postskills assessment and goal mastery, commitment for ongoing success	
Exit requirement: What method or process will be utilized to demonstrate the behavior academy exit criterion is met?	
Postskills assessment and goal mastery: What method will be utilized to conduct a postskill assessment of the students in this behavior academy?	
Commitment for ongoing success: What method, process, or both will be utilized to ensure students who meet the exit requirement develop a commitment for ongoing success utilizing learned skills in the future?	

Levels of Behavior Academy Application

We have found great success using the behavior academy structure as the vehicle to design and deliver effective behavior academies in schools. Each of the three core components in the behavior academy structure (initial session, ongoing sessions, and exit session) are essential in providing a comprehensive formalized targeted behavior intervention. However, as mentioned previously, we want to provide some guidance for educators or even a parent or guardian who would like to use behavior academies in a less formalized structure. To support these efforts, in this section, we outline the levels of application (formal and informal).

- ▶ Formal levels of application include the following.

  - All three components—(1) initial session, (2) ongoing sessions, (3) exit session—of the behavior academy structure must be fully in place with fidelity.

  - Behavior academy sessions should occur at least once a week for twenty-five minutes on an ongoing basis for at least six to eight weeks based on students' targeted goals.

  - Behavior academy sessions should be delivered in a small group or individualized fashion.

  - Ongoing sessions should be provided by a consistent person (typically a support provider such as a counselor, school psychologist, social worker, behavior specialist, and so on) based on targeted needs in a structured format.

  - Providers should progress monitor the effectiveness of sessions using student data.

- ▶ Informal levels of application include the following.

  - The informal implementation of behavior academies does not require all three components: (1) initial session, (2) ongoing sessions, (3) exit session.

  - Informal sessions may occur as needed rather than in a consistent weekly scheduled fashion.

  - Informal sessions can be delivered without any group-size restrictions. (They may include an entire class.)

  - Progress monitoring using student data is optional.

To elaborate further on informal levels of application, the informal implementation of behavior academies may be more centered around prevention, such as a classroom-based whole-class approach. We have also seen teachers pull small groups of students and provide reteaching opportunities. Most of the time, in these cases, we see the behavior rehearsal cards component of the behavior academy utilized in a variety of ways to help with prevention and some reteaching in the classroom setting. For example, if a teacher notices organization is an area of prevention need for the class, the teacher can utilize the organizational skills behavior rehearsal cards to help the entire class learn about targeted life skills and replacement behaviors for organization. The following are some additional examples.

- ▶ A teacher can pull one behavior rehearsal card a week to utilize for vocabulary development, application to scenarios, and practicing replacement behaviors as a class during a designated behavior prevention block of time (such as advisory, homeroom, social-emotional learning block, morning meeting time, and so on).

▶ A teacher can work with a small group of students to help give them replacement behavior to help with organization in the classroom once or twice a week during WIN (what I need now) intervention time or other intervention blocks.

▶ A group of teachers who collaborate and share students may identify a group of students who need some additional time and support with organization skills and decide what reteaching will look like by utilizing a behavior rehearsal card.

▶ A parent or guardian can use the behavior rehearsal cards to help teach and reinforce new life skills with their child at home.

▶ Teachers might utilize the behavior rehearsal cards as a classroom meeting topic once a week.

▶ Administrators can utilize a card a week over the announcements schoolwide as discussion points based on prevention needs schoolwide.

The possibilities of application and uses of the rehearsal cards are vast once you understand the thinking behind them.

To conclude this chapter, we want to offer three examples from a parent, an administrator, and a teacher to give context around what we mean by informal application of behavior academies as detailed in this section.

First, a parent shared that her son (five years old at the time) was really into playing with LEGO blocks. As he was building, the steps became more complicated, and some of the blocks were difficult to remove, so he started becoming frustrated and upset. We decided to apply our thinking of behavior academies to her son's scenario. So, she started an at-home behavior academy focusing on patience. Each week, she began to introduce a targeted life skill and corresponding replacement behaviors to help her son with patience. The first week, she began with the focus on help seeking ("Ask mommy or daddy for help when you are feeling frustrated."), and all week she reminded him and helped him practice how to ask for help. The second week, she added self-regulation (such as fun breathing exercises) to help calm himself down when the blocks frustrated him. The third week, she worked on identifying emotions and naming them, and so on. Each week, she taught and introduced a targeted life skill (replacement behaviors) to her five-year-old and created an environment where he could safely practice applying these newly learned skills. As you can see, she did not do the initial and exit session components of a formalized behavior academy, but she did use the thinking behind the ongoing behavior sessions to add to her son's inner toolkit. It was easy to do, and it worked!

To build on this informal application context, an administrator we support from an alternative education setting shared that he conducts his behavior academy ongoing sessions during a daily walk with students he mentors. For example, he shared that each day, he takes a walk with a different mentee and introduces a new targeted life skill and at least one replacement behavior around the area of focus, such as emotional regulation focusing on anger management replacement behaviors, among others. He said he does not have a separate classroom to conduct formal sessions in his school's design, but introducing these replacement behaviors while walking in nature has really helped with the students he serves. As you can see, he did not use the initial, exit, or monitoring tools during his delivery, but he has utilized the core thinking of teaching new targeted life skills to individual students or a small group of students on a weekly basis. It worked!

As a final teacher example of an informal application of behavior academies, see the lesson plan featured in figure 3.17 from a teacher who informally utilizes just the behavior rehearsal cards weekly with her students as prevention and some reteaching in small groups. As you can see on her lesson plan, she has identified the area of organization as an academic behavior need and focus for her class. She has integrated the teaching of targeted life skills, such as prioritizing and goal setting, into her morning meeting (whole class) and intervention (small group) structures.

Month: October Area of need: Organization (Teacher notes: Noticing incomplete and late work among the whole class and noticing a handful who are repeatedly struggling with organization) A small group of students repeatedly struggling with this area: J.F., T.R., L.W., and J.G.	**When:** During whole-class meetings and/or small group	**Which Behavior Rehearsal Card:** Follow the instructions on the card to define the targeted life skill, teach replacement behaviors, and hold classroom or small-group discussion around the scenario provided. If time permits, students can apply to student-developed scenarios.
Week 1	Classroom meeting (Monday)	Goal-setting behavior rehearsal card
Week 2	Classroom meeting (Monday) Intervention Block (Wednesday small group)	Prioritizing behavior rehearsal card Goal setting behavior rehearsal card (Review for small group)
Week 3	Classroom meeting (Monday)	Self-management behavior rehearsal card
Week 4	Classroom meeting (Monday) Intervention Block (Wednesday small group)	Preparedness behavior rehearsal card Prioritizing behavior rehearsal card (Review for small group)

FIGURE 3.17: Teacher lesson plan at a glance.

We provide these stories and the sample teacher lesson plan so you can better conceptualize the formal and informal application of behavior academies. As you read the next chapter on how to utilize our behavior rehearsal cards, you can envision what will be the best context for your twenty-five-minute ongoing sessions. In any case, you can see there are a variety of ways to make use of the thinking behind the behavior academies to teach productive behaviors.

In chapter 4, we provide the ready-made targeted behavior rehearsal cards for each of our eight behavior academies: Hands-Off Academy, Check-In Check-Out Academy, Civility Academy, Organizational Skills Academy, Social Skills Academy, Upstander Academy, Motivation Academy, and Emotional Regulation Academy as a teaching tool during the ongoing sessions of behavior academies (formal) or any range of informal application you decide to pursue.

Chapter 4

Behavior Academy Rehearsal Cards

A behavior intervention on a card.

—Jessica and John Hannigan

The behavior academy structure includes the initial session, the ongoing sessions, and the exit session, as explained in chapter 3 (page 25). However, one of the highest needs we hear from educators is not knowing what to teach during each behavior academy's ongoing sessions. This chapter provides an additional resource, the "what to teach" for each of our eight behavior academies to help support this need—using *behavior rehearsal cards*. Specifically, we want to provide a *behavior intervention on a card*, meaning an educator will have everything needed on each behavior rehearsal card to effectively provide a targeted behavior academy ongoing session in twenty-five minutes or less.

As a review, each of our eight behavior academies has eight targeted life skills with corresponding behavior rehearsal cards (totaling sixty-four to be exact), which you will find in this chapter. We want to provide at least eight weeks (one targeted life skill focus area per week) of content to ensure ongoing implementation and multiple data points of success over time. Remember, we want students to generalize these skills over time, so this is not a one- or two-time occurrence. Each behavior rehearsal card includes the targeted life skill and definition, two possible replacement behaviors to help students demonstrate each targeted life skill, a rehearsal and application scenario, and an opportunity for the students to create their own scenario for additional practice. Through these ready-made behavior rehearsal cards, we provide a quick, practical way to teach, reteach, or rehearse the identified targeted life skills for each behavior academy.

In this chapter, you will find behavior rehearsal cards for use during the behavior academy ongoing sessions, for each of the following eight behavior academies. (Visit **www.SolutionTree.com/behavior/BA** and enter the unique access code found on the inside front cover to access the exclusive online reproducibles from this chapter.)

1. Hands-Off Academy (page 58)

2. Check-In Check-Out Academy (page 68)

3. Civility Academy (page 77)

4. Organizational Skills Academy (page 86)

5. Social Skills Academy (page 95)

6. Upstander Academy (page 104)

7. Motivation Academy (page 113)

8. Emotional Regulation Academy (page 122)

The ultimate outcome of the behavior academy ongoing sessions is for students to develop an *inner life-skills toolkit*. In other words, it is for students to develop automatic productive habits they can pull from and generalize in school and life, replacing unproductive behaviors. You can utilize the behavior rehearsal cards with students in a variety of ways: print them, cut them out, and put them onto rings for younger students; cut and paste them into a journal or folder for students to use; or print them in their full format (inclusive of all eight targeted life skills) for students to reference.

Although we provide our most popular tried-and-tested replacement behaviors based on imagery and visualization for the behavior rehearsal cards to help students demonstrate the targeted life skills aligned with each respective behavior academy, this does not mean you cannot add additional replacement behaviors when necessary. We want to change your thinking about the design and implementation of a behavior intervention by providing an approach that is consistent, effective, and practical.

Some educators use the behavior rehearsal cards as stand-alone lessons, as we recommend, since all the necessary content is there to hold an effective ongoing session. Others build on additional connections to the targeted skill and replacement behaviors by supplementing using pictures, video clips, books or stories, existing district-adopted behavior lessons or curriculum, and so on, which would have to be prepared prior to a session. The main point is to maintain the targetedness while keeping it practical and efficient (short but effective, based on the attention span of the students involved) so that it is easy for students to generalize what you are teaching them. We ultimately want students to instinctively pull from their inner life-skills toolkit when faced with challenging situations independently, whether an adult is there or not.

Hands-Off Academy Behavior Rehearsal Cards

Hands-Off Academy was designed to help students struggling to keep their hands to themselves when they are angry or perceive a situation to be unfair. See the behavior academy definition, eight targeted life skills, and replacement behaviors that align with Hands-Off Academy, along with the corresponding behavior rehearsal cards (see table 4.1 and figure 4.1, page 60).

TABLE 4.1: Hands-Off Academy At-A-Glance

Behavior Academy	Eight Targeted Life Skills	Replacement Behaviors
Hands-Off Academy	**Self-reflection:** The ability to look inward to understand how your thoughts, feelings, and behaviors impact your overall behavior and personal growth	Three Rs (<u>r</u>ewind, <u>r</u>eplay, <u>r</u>edo) Voice memo to self
	Conflict resolution: The ability to resolve disagreements and find solutions in a peaceful and constructive manner without resorting to aggressive behaviors	Thought cloud Win-win scenario thinking
	Impulse control: The ability to stop and think about the consequences of your actions in the heat of the moment before acting impulsively	Imaginary pause button (or stop sign) Remove myself
	Identifying emotional triggers: The ability to recognize your body's reactions and understand the situations and experiences that lead to these negative reactions and behaviors	Pinpoint your body's reactions Name and track the trigger
	Self-regulation: The ability to demonstrate awareness of your thoughts and emotions and how to manage them in a productive manner during challenging situations	Assuring self-talk Deep breathing (box breathing)
	Accountability: The ability to take responsibility for one's actions, decisions, and consequences while taking steps to improve	Own it and apologize Accountability self-check
	Help seeking: The ability to recognize and actively seek support and guidance from trusted individuals when faced with difficulties or challenges	Reach out to someone you trust (adult) Talk back to your inner voice
	Communication (verbal and nonverbal): The ability to actively listen and use both verbal (using words) and nonverbal (body language, facial expressions, gestures) methods to express thoughts and feelings in a positive manner	Use my voice Self-scan

Targeted life skill: SELF-REFLECTION

Hands-Off Academy

Definition: The ability to look inward to understand how your thoughts, feelings, and behaviors impact your overall behavior and personal growth

Replacement behaviors:

Three Rs (rewind, replay, redo)—Imagine the incident you experienced as a short video you can play in your head. Imagine having the ability to rewind, replay, and redo as many times as you need. Imagine where you were, where the other person was (or people were), what you said or did, what they said or did, how it made you feel, and how you responded.

Now, use the 3Rs. **R**ewind the incident, and **r**eplay it in your head or talk through it out loud. Then, **r**edo the part of the incident where things went wrong. Think about one or two ways you would change (redo) your response in the future, such as taking back your reaction and use of hands-on behavior.

Voice memo to self—Imagine yourself using a voice memo app on your phone or device. A voice memo is usually a short recording of yourself speaking to yourself in a way that allows you to express your feelings and self-reflect in a safe place. Act like you are recording a short voice memo (message) to yourself about the incident and what you learned from it. Allow yourself to replay scenes from this incident and the challenges you faced. Pay close attention to how you felt in these moments. What emotions did you experience? How did your body feel? Speak each thought as it comes, focusing on honesty and openness. As you finish, imagine wrapping up your thoughts like the end of a story. Lastly, picture yourself in the future, listening back to your voice memo. What would you tell yourself that may help you in the future? Remember, you are not actually recording this on a device but using this as an exercise to self-reflect.

Rehearsal and application scenario:

Abel and Jared were involved in a fight during a football game disagreement. While Jared took some time to reflect on the fight and what he could have done instead to solve the problem, Abel did not think twice about his role in the fight.

Wrong way to respond? Right way to respond?

Student-created scenario:

Wrong way to respond? Right way to respond?

Targeted life skill: **CONFLICT RESOLUTION**

Hands-Off Academy

Definition: The ability to resolve disagreements and find solutions in a peaceful and constructive manner without resorting to aggressive behaviors

Replacement behaviors:

Thought cloud—A *thought cloud* is a visual representation of a person's thoughts and feelings; some good, some not so good. Think of a recent conflict with another student and describe what happened. Now, imagine a thought cloud above each person's head in the conflict, including your own. These thought clouds should contain what each person might be thinking or feeling but not saying out loud. Consider using a thought cloud to capture your inappropriate responses to conflict. A thought cloud will be a good place to store your negative thoughts and feelings while you calm down and respond appropriately.

Now, consider the other person in the conflict and imagine their thought cloud. What misunderstandings or assumptions might be fueling this conflict? Think of ways to address the concerns and feelings in the thought clouds.

Win-win scenario thinking—Win-win scenario thinking encourages you to consider solutions where both people in the conflict can get their needs met (win-win). Choose a conflict scenario that is relevant to you. Reflect on those involved in the conflict and imagine the conflict unfolding. What are the people saying? How are they feeling? What do they want? What is their body language showing? Imagine each expressing their feelings and needs.

Now imagine what would happen if both people in the conflict responded inappropriately (that is a lose-lose scenario). For example, both can get into trouble, lose privileges, lose trust, and so on.

Now imagine both people in the conflict-winning (win-win) scenario. What does a win look like for you? What does a win look like for the other person? When you find yourself in these scenarios, use win-win scenario thinking to push yourself to think of a better way to respond.

Rehearsal and application scenario:

Sam is struggling getting along with another student in one of his classes named Marty. Marty and Sam are constantly making mean comments to each other. It has gone too far, and now the only way Sam thinks he can resolve the conflict is by using his hands to make it stop.

Wrong way to respond? Right way to respond?

Student-created scenario:

Wrong way to respond? Right way to respond?

FIGURE 4.1: Hands-Off Academy behavior rehearsal cards.

continued →

Targeted life skill: IMPULSE CONTROL

Hands-Off Academy

Definition: The ability to stop and think about the consequences of your actions in the heat of the moment before acting impulsively

Replacement behaviors:

Imaginary pause button (or stop sign)—A pause button and a stop sign are signals that remind us to automatically pause or stop for a designated amount of time. Practice imagining a pause button (or stop sign) in your brain when you feel yourself getting upset or angry and wanting to resort to hands-on behaviors. The pause button (or stop sign) will help you catch yourself when you are getting upset and angry before you respond.

Remove myself—Imagine ways to remove yourself from a situation when you feel yourself becoming upset or angry. Imagine the roadblocks in your way of removing yourself. For example, maybe a friend tells you not to leave so you do not look afraid or weak. Or bystanders are encouraging you to engage in a fight. How would you respond to them and remove yourself anyway? Pay close attention to what you are thinking and feeling in these situations. Imagine yourself walking away without turning around and making comments to the person upsetting you or making you angry. This will help you physically remove yourself in future situations just like you imagined.

Rehearsal and application scenario:

During lunch, Jeff accidentally bumped into Maddox, spilling his food all over Maddox's new shirt. Maddox, already having a bad day and feeling embarrassed, pushed Jeff to get back at him, which started a fight between the two. Bystanders were encouraging the students to fight. In a later discussion with the administration, it was discovered that a past unresolved incident between the boys had impacted this event.

Wrong way to respond? Right way to respond?

Student-created scenario:

Wrong way to respond? Right way to respond?

IDENTIFYING EMOTIONAL TRIGGERS

Targeted life skill:

Hands-Off Academy

Definition: The ability to recognize your body's reactions and understand the situations and experiences that lead to these negative reactions and behaviors

Replacement behaviors:

Pinpoint your body's reactions—Recall a recent situation that resulted in a strong emotional response (where you felt extremely upset or angry at a person). Notice the emotions that surface. Is it anger, sadness, frustration, anxiety? Name the emotion.

Now, shift your focus to your body's response. Where in your body do you feel a response? Is it a tightness in your chest, a knot in your stomach, or tension in your shoulders? Or are your hands clenched? Is your breathing fast?

There is a connection between the physical sensations and the emotion you have named. For example, "When I feel anxious, my stomach knots up," or "When I'm angry, my fists clench." Naming your emotions and being aware of your body's reactions will help you pinpoint when you are getting angry or upset.

Imagine pinpointing something you are looking for on a map, but instead of a map, you are pinpointing your body's reaction. This will help you identify when you are angry and upset and work on calming yourself down before your body's reactions get bigger.

Name and track the trigger—Recall a recent situation where you felt a strong emotion. Visualize this event in detail, like watching a movie in your mind, and examine the moment you first felt the emotional change. Give a name to this trigger. This could be a single word or a short phrase that sums up the essence of the trigger (such as *criticism, exclusion, failure,* or *overwhelmed* to name a few).

Explore how your body felt at that moment. Did your heart rate increase? Did you feel hot or cold? Any tension in specific body parts? Identify the emotions you felt. Was it anger, sadness, anxiety, or something else? Think about why this particular event or detail triggered you. How does this trigger relate to your current emotions and behaviors? Track how often this is triggering you and when. Naming and tracking your triggers (knowing what your triggers are) will help you control your response to these strong emotions.

Rehearsal and application scenario:

Matt says something hurtful and embarrassing to Jean in front of other students and everyone begins to laugh at him. Jean feels himself becoming hot. Jean wants to show Matt how bad it made him feel by embarrassing Matt in front of his other friends and pushing him to the ground.

Wrong way to respond? Right way to respond?

Student-created scenario:

Wrong way to respond? Right way to respond?

continued →

Targeted life skill: SELF-REGULATION

Hands-Off Academy

Definition: The ability to demonstrate awareness of your thoughts and emotions and how to manage them in a productive manner during challenging situations

Replacement behaviors:

Assuring self-talk—Self-talk in itself can sometimes be negative and/or positive. Assuring self-talk is helping you keep how you speak to yourself, especially in an upsetting situation focused on the positive. For example, when you are feeling upset or angry, keep telling (assuring) yourself it is going to be OK, your emotions are going to pass, and there is a better way. This will help you be aware of what is going on and calm yourself down.

Deep breathing (box breathing)—Visualize the sides of a square or box as you go through each step. For example, picture a line being drawn upward as you inhale, a line being drawn to the right as you hold, a line being drawn downward as you exhale, and a line being drawn to the left as you hold again.

1. **Close your eyes.** This will help you focus on your breathing and reduce distractions.

2. **Exhale.** Begin by exhaling completely through your mouth to empty your lungs.

3. **Inhale for a count of four.** Slowly and deeply inhale through your nose for a count of four. Focus on the air filling your lungs.

4. **Hold your breath for a count of four.** After you've taken a full breath in, hold it for a count of four.

5. **Exhale for a count of four.** Exhale through your mouth for a count of 4, releasing the air from your lungs.

6. **Hold your lungs empty for a count of 4.** After you've exhaled completely, pause and keep your lungs empty for another count of four.

Rehearsal and application scenario:

Amid the chatter of the school hallway, Jake accused Alex of spreading false rumors about him. Alex, embarrassed and furious, shoved Jake hard against the lockers. Without hesitation, Jake retaliated with a swift punch to Alex's jaw. The echoing noise instantly drew a crowd of shocked students.

Wrong way to respond? Right way to respond?

Student-created scenario:

Wrong way to respond? Right way to respond?

Targeted life skill: ACCOUNTABILITY

Hands-Off Academy

Definition: The ability to take responsibility for one's actions, decisions, and consequences while taking steps to improve

Replacement behaviors:

Own it and apologize—Visualize yourself owning it (owning your actions) to yourself and to the other person you impacted. Imagine the possibility the person may or may not be responsive. Be prepared to accept that may be a possible response from them. Practice acknowledging and providing an authentic apology that addresses the following and then do it.

1. **Recognize and acknowledge:** Clearly state what you did wrong.

2. **Accept responsibility:** Own your actions and the impact they've had.

3. **State what you learned:** Assure you will not do this again in the future and the steps you are taking to prevent it from happening again.

4. **Have a plan to improve next time:** Make a plan and use it in the future if you find yourself in this type of scenario again: "Next time, I will _____ instead of putting my hands on someone else. One way I can follow through on my plan is by _____."

Accountability self-check—It will be difficult to learn and grow from your actions if you do not take accountability for them. For example, imagine the situation that got you here. How are you going to stop yourself from blaming others and conduct a quick accountability self-check to help you for the now and the future?

Answer the two following quick questions with only one rule in mind. You cannot answer shifting the blame to anyone else. This does not mean the other person or people did not do anything wrong; it just means you are practicing taking a true accountability self-check of your part in the incident so you do not find yourself in this situation in the future.

1. What was my part in this incident?

2. What am I going to do in the future to prevent this from happening again?

Rehearsal and application scenario:

Val gets into a pushing match with Rod during break. When asked by an adult what happened, Val keeps insisting she did not do anything and continuously blames Rod for bumping into her on purpose. She refuses to apologize.

Wrong way to respond? Right way to respond?

Student-created scenario:

Wrong way to respond? Right way to respond?

continued →

Targeted life skill: **HELP SEEKING**

Hands-Off Academy

Definition: The ability to recognize and actively seek support and guidance from trusted individuals when faced with difficulties or challenges

Replacement behaviors:

Reach out to someone you trust (adult)— Imagine a situation where you felt that you needed help or support. Visualize a trusted adult in your life (a parent, teacher, counselor, or family friend). Focus on why you trust this person. Imagine walking up to this trusted adult, and visualize starting a conversation. Think about what words you would use to express your needs. You might say something like, "I'm feeling really overwhelmed with a situation at school, and I don't know what to do. Can I talk to you about it?" Imagine the trusted adult listening carefully, showing concern, and offering support. Think about how you might feel after getting help: relieved, understood, supported, and so on. After the visualization: How did it feel to imagine this scenario? What parts were easy or hard to visualize?

Talk back to your inner voice—Everyone has an inner dialogue that can be both positive and negative. It's normal to have doubts and fears, but it's important to recognize when these thoughts are unhelpful.

Now, imagine a scenario where you are facing a challenge or problem. Pay attention to your inner voice. What is it saying? Is it discouraging or critical? Recognize these thoughts. Now, prepare yourself to transform this inner dialogue and imagine a supportive, understanding voice. This could be your own voice or someone you trust and respect. What would this helpful voice say in this situation?

Imagine a conversation with this helpful inner voice. Express your concerns and listen to the responses from this supportive voice. This voice should offer encouragement and practical advice and remind you of your past successes and strengths.

Next, visualize taking the step of seeking help from someone you trust: a teacher, friend, counselor, or family member. Imagine how you would approach this person and what you would say. How did it feel talking to a helpful inner voice? What insights did you gain about seeking help?

Rehearsal and application scenario:

You are being pressured into meeting up with someone to fight after school. You do not want to fight but you also do not want to look like you are afraid in front of your peers.

Wrong way to respond? Right way to respond?

Student-created scenario:

Wrong way to respond? Right way to respond?

Targeted life skill: COMMUNICATION (verbal and nonverbal)

Hands-Off Academy

Definition: The ability to actively listen and use both verbal (using words) and nonverbal (body language, facial expressions, gestures) methods to express thoughts and feelings in a positive manner

Replacement behaviors:

Use my voice—Imagine a specific conflict arising. For example, you could imagine someone disagreeing with your opinion or calling you a name. Pay attention to how you feel in this imagined scenario and how you will communicate. Are you frustrated, angry, or anxious? What will you share with the person or people upsetting you?

Now, imagine responding to the conflict, emphasizing the use of a calm and steady voice. Mentally practice phrases like, "I do not like what you said," "Please stop calling me that," and "Your words are upsetting me" instead of using hands-on behavior. The tone should be assertive yet respectful.

Self-scan—When you scan something, you capture and store the image of something. Take a self-scan of what you are portraying (communicating) to others (nonverbally). Self-scan your body all the way up to your face, readjust, and consciously relax and focus on neutral body language. For example, if you catch yourself with clenched fists, relax your hands or put them in your lap; if you notice intense eye contact, soften your gaze or look away; or if you have a tense face, relax your facial muscles.

Rehearsal and application scenario:

During lunch, Jasmine accused Alexandra of spreading rumors about her and her friends. Alexandra, rolled her eyes and shot back, "Maybe they're true!" They stood inches apart, eyes locked and fists clenched. The tension grew more intense as classmates circled around, expecting a fight.

Wrong way to respond? Right way to respond?

Student-created scenario:

Wrong way to respond? Right way to respond?

Check-In Check-Out Academy Behavior Rehearsal Cards

Check-In Check-Out Academy is designed for students struggling with repeated minor classroom misbehaviors. See the eight targeted life skills that align with Check-In Check-Out Academy along with the corresponding behavior rehearsal cards (see table 4.2 and figure 4.2).

TABLE 4.2: Check-In Check-Out Academy At-A-Glance

Behavior Academy	Eight Targeted Life Skills	Replacement Behaviors
Check-In Check-Out Academy	**Respect for others:** The ability to acknowledge the feelings, emotions, rights, differences, and efforts of others while maintaining positive interactions	Switch places Invisible boundary line
	Active listening: The ability to give your full attention to hear what someone is saying to you without thinking about your response, so you can fully comprehend what they are saying (that is, their feelings, needs, ideas, emotions, intentions)	Headphones on (or listening ears on) Magnifying glass
	Self-control: The ability to manage and regulate your behaviors by stopping and considering different choices and outcomes for the purpose of selecting the most appropriate responses	Boss of your own feelings (or superhero inside) Driving a car
	Self-discipline: The ability to control one's own actions and behaviors while keeping the long-term goals in mind despite potential distractions, setbacks, and short-term temptations	Inner coach Secret tool in a video game
	Receptive to feedback: The ability and willingness to listen and accept input from others about your behavior and being open-minded to suggestions that help you improve, even if it is not what you were hoping to hear	Put down the shield Seek clarification (information-seeking questions)
	Self-monitoring: The ability to closely pay attention, observe, and keep track of what works for you to improve your behaviors and actions	Detective of your own actions Special inner flashlight
	Persistence: The ability to stick to your set goals, adapt your behaviors and actions when needed, and learn from challenges or obstacles	The personal fan club Climbing the ladder
	Responsible decision making: The ability to make good choices about your behavior and learn from your choices to make better decisions in the future	Time machine (If, then) Attach a feeling to the action

Targeted life skill: **RESPECT FOR OTHERS**

Check-In Check-Out Academy

Definition: The ability to acknowledge the feelings, emotions, rights, differences, and efforts of others while maintaining positive interactions

Replacement behaviors:

Switch places—Imagine yourself physically or emotionally switching places with another person. For example, imagine if you were the teacher and a student was constantly giving you a difficult time.

When you catch yourself showing disrespectful behaviors in class, imagine switching places with the person and consider if you would keep doing it. As the teacher in this scenario: How would you feel in their place? What might be going through your mind? What would you want others to do or say if you were in this situation?

Now switch back to your own perspective. How does this experience change the way you would act or respond in real life? Whenever you face a conflict or a social dilemma, pause and imagine switching places with the other person.

Invisible boundary line—Respecting others can be thought of as being aware of an invisible line. This line represents the boundary between behavior that is respectful and behavior that is not. Now, imagine an invisible line in front of you. This line separates respectful behavior (on one side) from disrespectful behavior (on the other). Imagine complimenting someone. See yourself standing on the respectful side of the line. Now, imagine saying something hurtful. Notice how you step over the line into the disrespectful area. Pay attention to how you feel when you are on each side of the line.

Rehearsal and application scenario:

Noah continues to repeatedly blurt out and interrupt his teacher during her lesson, disregarding her efforts to teach a lesson. When redirected, he responds in a disrespectful way.

Wrong way to respond? Right way to respond?

Student-created scenario:

Wrong way to respond? Right way to respond?

FIGURE 4.2: Check-In Check-Out Academy behavior rehearsal cards. continued ➝

Targeted life skill: **ACTIVE LISTENING**

Check-In Check-Out Academy

Definition: The ability to give your full attention to hear what someone is saying to you without thinking about your response so you can fully comprehend what they are saying (that is, their feelings, needs, ideas, emotions, intentions)

Replacement behaviors:

Headphones on (or listening ears on)—Active listening means paying full attention to someone when they are speaking. It's not just about hearing their words but also understanding what they mean. Imagine you have a special pair of headphones. These aren't just any headphones, but special ones designed for deep listening. Imagine you are gently placing these headphones over your ears. They fit perfectly and make you feel focused and calm. When these headphones are on, they have a special power—these headphones help you to listen not just to the words that people say but also to the feelings and ideas behind those words. Imagine situations where you would put these headphones on; for example, when a teacher is giving instructions, when a friend is sharing a story, or when a parent is asking you to do something. Imagine you are sitting with a friend or a family member, and they are talking to you about something important to them. With your active-listening headphones on, notice how you focus on their words. Imagine yourself being really interested in what they are saying, nodding your head, and making eye contact.

Magnifying glass—Just as a magnifying glass helps us see things more clearly and in greater detail, we can use one as a symbol for listening more closely and attentively. When we hold our mental magnifying glass up to someone's words, we focus intently on what they say. Visualize using your mental magnifying glass to focus on the words of your teacher giving instructions or a family member sharing something important. Notice not just the content of what's being said but also the tone, pace, and emotion. Use your magnifying glass whenever you need to give your full attention to focus on what someone is saying.

Rehearsal and application scenario:

During a private discussion aimed at improving his behavior, Emmett seemed disengaged from his teacher's words. He consistently responded with brief, one-word answers, kept his arms crossed, and looked distracted throughout.

Wrong way to respond? Right way to respond?

Student-created scenario:

Wrong way to respond? Right way to respond?

Targeted life skill: **SELF-CONTROL**

Check-In Check-Out Academy

Definition: The ability to manage and regulate your behaviors by stopping and considering different choices and outcomes for the purpose of selecting the most appropriate responses

Replacement behaviors:

Boss of your own feelings (or superhero inside)—Name yourself the boss (or superhero inside) and put yourself in charge of your behavior. Visualize your inner boss (or superhero) when faced with a difficult situation. How would the boss (or superhero) version handle it?

Driving a car—Visualize yourself driving a car as a metaphor for demonstrating self-control during challenging situations in life. Think of the car as yourself and the steering wheel as your self-control. As the driver, you have control of the steering wheel. When faced with an obstacle or a tough situation, you decide which way to turn, how fast to go, or whether to stop. Sometimes, the road is smooth and clear; other times, it's filled with obstacles, sharp turns, and unexpected situations. Your self-control helps you navigate these challenges and keeps you on track. If you turn the wheel sharply without thinking, you might go off course.

Rehearsal and application scenario:

James is constantly making disruptive noises, getting out of his seat and walking around, and talking to other classmates during class. James ignores his teacher's efforts to redirect him.

Wrong way to respond? Right way to respond?

Student-created scenario:

Wrong way to respond? Right way to respond?

continued →

Targeted life skill: **SELF-DISCIPLINE**

Check-In Check-Out Academy

Definition: The ability to control one's own actions and behaviors while keeping the long-term goals in mind despite potential distractions, setbacks, and short-term temptations

Replacement behaviors:

Inner coach—Activate (turn on) your inner coach when you are feeling yourself getting off track. Your inner coach is a supportive, wise, and motivating figure within you who guides you through challenges and helps you stay on track. It is a wise mentor, a favorite teacher, a successful version of yourself in the future, or even a fictional character known for their discipline and wisdom.

Imagine a scenario where you're facing a challenge or temptation. Let your inner coach step in. Mentally express your challenge to your inner coach. Imagine how your inner coach would respond. What advice or encouragement would they offer? Take these words to heart. Feel the support and guidance. Visualize yourself following the coach's advice and overcoming the challenge. Notice any feelings of confidence, determination, or calm that arise.

Throughout your day, remind yourself of your inner coach's advice. In moments of challenge, pause and think, "What would my inner coach say?"

Secret tool in a video game—Imagine you are playing a video game. In this game, you have a secret tool that's extremely powerful. It's not a weapon or an item but an internal skill that can significantly influence the outcome of the game.

For example, this secret tool may be self-discipline. Just like in real life, players have the ability to choose their actions in the game. Sometimes, there are easier and tempting shortcuts, but they might come at a cost. The secret tool of self-discipline helps you resist these shortcuts and make choices that help you in the long run. Just like any skill in a video game, self-discipline gets stronger with practice.

Rehearsal and application scenario:

Oliver's friend Zad keeps trying to engage in conversation during work time. Oliver is trying to stay on task but also wants to be friends with Zad so he doesn't want to ignore him.

Wrong way to respond? Right way to respond?

Student-created scenario:

Wrong way to respond? Right way to respond?

Targeted life skill: RECEPTIVE TO FEEDBACK

Check-In Check-Out Academy

Definition: The ability and willingness to listen and accept input from others about your behavior and being open-minded to suggestions that help you improve, even if it is not what you were hoping to hear

Replacement behaviors:

Put down the shield—Imagine that you are holding a large, heavy shield in front of you. This shield represents your defenses (automatic reactions that might make you feel defensive, resistant, or hurt when hearing feedback). Feel the weight of the shield. The shield might feel heavy and burdensome, representing the energy and effort it takes to always be on the defensive.

Now, examine the shield. Look closely at this shield. Is it battered with marks from past criticisms or negative feedback? Does it have any inscriptions or words that stand out, like "Not good enough" or "Failure?" Recognizing these can help you understand the baggage you might carry regarding feedback.

Next, lower the shield. Visualize yourself slowly lowering the shield to the ground, setting it aside. As you do this, feel the lightness and relief of not having to carry or hold up that weight any longer.

Seek clarification (information-seeking questions)—Visualize a situation where you will receive feedback on an assignment, a piece of work, or a performance. This could be in a classroom setting, a one-on-one meeting with a teacher, or while working on a group project. Let the person provide feedback that is constructive and specific but also challenging. Recognize your initial emotional response. This might include feelings of disappointment, defensiveness, confusion, or anxiety. It's important to understand that these feelings are normal.

Now, imagine taking a deep breath and consciously shifting your mindset from a defensive stance to one of openness and curiosity. Visualize yourself asking questions to clarify the feedback, such as: "Could you give me an example of where I could improve?" or "What specific steps can I take to do better next time?" These questions should be aimed at understanding the feedback more clearly, not at defending yourself.

Finally, visualize identifying key points and how to apply this feedback in your next project, assignment, or study session.

Rehearsal and application scenario:

Ava gets defensive when her teacher gives her feedback about her behavior during class. Ava shuts down and stops listening. She feels like no one wants to help her.

Wrong way to respond? Right way to respond?

Student-created scenario:

Wrong way to respond? Right way to respond?

continued →

Definition: The ability to closely pay attention, observe, and keep track of what works for you to improve your behaviors and actions

Replacement behaviors:

Detective of your own actions—Act like a detective of your own actions. Pay close attention to details and clues (track your actions and habits); gather evidence and analyze it to help you improve. Are there specific times when you are most productive? When do you procrastinate the most?

Special inner flashlight—Imagine you have a special inner flashlight you can turn on to illuminate (highlight) your actions and behaviors clearly to help you stay on track. This flashlight represents your self-monitoring and ability to understand and reflect on your behaviors. It allows you to see things clearly and make informed decisions.

Now, adjust the beam. Just like a real flashlight can have a focused beam or a broad illumination (light), you can adjust your actions and behaviors. A narrow focus might help examine a single behavior deeply, while a broader focus can help you understand how multiple behaviors fit together in your life.

Next, explore with the light. Now that you have your flashlight on, explore your inner space. What behaviors do you see? Are there actions you're proud of? Are there things you'd like to change?

Rehearsal and application scenario:

During class, Mrs. James's students were engaged in group discussions about their projects. While most were focused on their own tasks, Maliki's attention darted from group to group, criticizing their behaviors and listening in on their conversations. Consumed by the activities of his peers, he failed to realize that he hadn't contributed a single idea to his own group's project.

Wrong way to respond? Right way to respond?

Student-created scenario:

Wrong way to respond? Right way to respond?

Targeted life skill: **PERSISTENCE**

Check-In Check-Out Academy

Definition: The ability to stick to your set goals, adapt your behaviors and actions when needed, and learn from challenges or obstacles

Replacement behaviors:

The personal fan club—Imagine walking into a stadium. As you get farther in, you start to recognize the people in the crowd. It's everyone who's ever believed in you—family, friends, teachers, coaches, mentors—even your future self! Every person is there, cheering you on and holding signs. Focus on these signs, which read, "You can do this!" "Keep going!" and "We believe in you!" Cheer on, encourage, and celebrate yourself and all your wins (big or small).

Climbing the ladder—Imagine climbing a ladder one rung at a time. Each rung represents a task or challenge. You can't skip rungs on a ladder without risking a fall. It's OK to rest on a rung when you feel tired or overwhelmed. Just as a person can pause on a rung to catch their breath, students can take a break but should then continue climbing. Compare your growth from where you are to how you started.

Rehearsal and application scenario:

Scott feels like it will be impossible to meet his daily goals in class. He is so overwhelmed and keeps thinking to himself, "It is not worth the effort. I might as well not do it at all."

Wrong way to respond? Right way to respond?

Student-created scenario:

Wrong way to respond? Right way to respond?

continued →

Targeted life skill: RESPONSIBLE DECISION MAKING

Check-In Check-Out Academy

Definition: The ability to make good choices about your behavior and learn from your choices to make better decisions in the future

Replacement behaviors:

Time machine (If, then)—Before engaging in an action, put yourself in an imaginary time machine to time travel into the future. Say, "If I do _____ (action), then _____ (result) is what I see happening." This will help you make a good choice, knowing what is going to happen.

Attach a feeling to the action—Before engaging in an action, remind yourself what negative feelings may also come from that action.

First, identify the action. Start by discussing some poor actions or behaviors you have demonstrated in class. Examples could be getting off task, interrupting a teacher, talking while the teacher is talking, and getting out of your seat. Next, attach the feeling. (How did the consequences of these actions make you feel?)

Rehearsal and application scenario:

Alex forgot to bring his daily check form to his teacher and continuously interrupted class with inappropriate comments. He figured he already was not going to meet his daily goals since he forgot his form, so why even try?

Wrong way to respond? Right way to respond?

Student-created scenario:

Wrong way to respond? Right way to respond?

Civility Academy Behavior Rehearsal Cards

Civility Academy is designed for students struggling to maintain civil discourse with other peers and adults who may have different points of view. See the eight targeted life skills that align with Civility Academy along with the corresponding behavior rehearsal cards (see table 4.3 and figure 4.3, page 78).

TABLE 4.3: Civility Academy At-A-Glance

Behavior Academy	Eight Targeted Life Skills	Replacement Behaviors
Civility Academy	**Empathic listening:** The ability to put yourself in someone else's position while seeking to understand their emotions, thoughts, and experiences from their viewpoint in a nonjudgmental way	Wait time Paraphrase
	Integrity: The ability to consistently demonstrate honesty and having the courage to do the right thing even when it feels challenging	Give advice to a character in a movie Listen to your inner voice
	Responsibility: The ability to accept the consequences of your actions and work toward making things right	Future projection Move the weight
	Social and cultural awareness: The ability to understand and appreciate one's personal social identity and cultural differences	Garden (different flowers all grow together) Fill in the blanks
	Coexisting: The ability to accept other people's ideas, beliefs, and perspectives that do not align with yours and to be in the same space at the same time peacefully	Agree to disagree Pieces of a jigsaw puzzle
	Open-minded: The ability to admit what you do not know and the willingness to learn about new ideas and points of view in the interest of demonstrating tolerance and acceptance	Two sides of a coin Three As (<u>a</u>sk questions, <u>a</u>void becoming defensive, <u>a</u>ccept change)
	Perspective taking: The ability to put oneself in someone else's position or situation while considering how their experiences have influenced them	Zoom out (beyond your perspective) Narrate it from another person's standpoint
	Compassion: The ability to understand and share the feelings of another who is having a difficult time *and* the desire to offer help and support, with a willingness to do something about it	Kind acts daily Offer help

Targeted life skill: **EMPATHIC LISTENING**

Civility Academy

Definition: The ability to put yourself in someone else's position while seeking to understand their emotions, thoughts, and experiences from their viewpoint in a nonjudgmental way

Replacement behaviors:

Wait time—Visualize yourself sitting, and opposite of you is a friend, classmate, or family member. They are sharing something important to them—it could be a problem, a feeling, or an experience they've had. They are looking for understanding, not just a response. As they finish a point, instead of jumping in with your response, count slowly to three to five in your mind.

During this time, maintain eye contact and show that you are thoughtfully listening. This pause is your wait time. Use this time to really absorb what's been said. Think about the emotions behind the words. Reflect on why this might be significant to them.

After the wait time, respond. Your response should show that you've truly listened. It could be a reflective statement, a validating comment, or an open-ended question to encourage them to share more. Watch how the other person reacts to your response. Often, they will feel more understood and valued, leading to a deeper, more meaningful conversation.

The conversation continues in this rhythm, with you intentionally implementing wait time after each speaking turn.

Paraphrase—Paraphrasing words involves reflecting the emotions behind those words. For example:

Original statement: "I felt hurt when you made that comment about my religion."

Paraphrased statement: "You felt upset because I made an insensitive comment about your religion."

Use the following steps to paraphrase.

1. Listen actively. Be present, avoid interrupting, and give your full attention.

2. Pause before responding. After the speaker has finished, take a moment to process what was said.

3. Rephrase without adding. Use different words but maintain the original meaning. Avoid adding personal opinions or interpretations.

4. Check for understanding. After paraphrasing, ask the speaker if your interpretation was accurate.

Rehearsal and application scenario:

TJ made insensitive remarks to Eli regarding his faith. The administrator orchestrates a constructive dialogue between the two students to foster understanding. However, TJ seems disinterested in Eli's feelings about the comments and frequently cuts him off.

Wrong way to respond? Right way to respond?

Student-created scenario:

Wrong way to respond? Right way to respond?

Targeted life skill: INTEGRITY

Civility Academy

Definition: The ability to consistently demonstrate honesty and having the courage to do the right thing even when it feels challenging

Replacement behaviors:

Give advice to a character in a movie—Imagine you are the friend of a main character in a movie who is making some poor choices. Identify the decisions this main character is making that are hurtful to others. As a friend to the main character, what advice would you give? How can the main character demonstrate integrity in this situation? Think deeply about the best course of action, the consequences of each choice, and the value of integrity as you give advice.

Listen to your inner voice—Be in tune and pay attention to your inner voice telling you to do the right thing. Imagine a scenario where you face a moral or ethical dilemma where you need to choose between an easy option and the right option. Imagine the feelings and perspectives of everyone involved in the scenario. Imagine responding to the situation. Hear your own voice advocating for what is right and fair. Listen carefully to what your inner voice says, picturing it as a guide or mentor.

Rehearsal and application scenario:

David consistently denies to the school officials that he wrote a hurtful note found near his desk about Jeremy, a student he had a heated argument with earlier in class. Despite being the author of the note, David maintains his innocence.

Wrong way to respond? Right way to respond?

Student-created scenario:

Wrong way to respond? Right way to respond?

FIGURE 4.3: Civility Academy behavior rehearsal cards.

continued →

Targeted life skill: RESPONSIBILITY

Civility Academy

Definition: The ability to accept the consequences of your actions and work toward making things right

Replacement behaviors:

Future projection—Visualize your future of being consistently responsible for your actions and willingness to make things right. How will this help your life and relationships in a week? In a month? In a year? Now, visualize your future if you are consistently not responsible for your actions and unwilling to make things right. How will this impact your life and relationships in a week? In a month? In a year?

Move the weight—Visualize yourself holding a heavy object near your chest. The heavy object weighs a lot and represents a time when you did not take responsibility—your shame and lack of honesty regarding your actions. By not taking responsibility and blaming others, over time, the object's weight becomes heavier to carry.

Now imagine yourself taking responsibility for your actions and letting an adult help you learn how to do better when you are in that situation again. Imagine the pressure of the weight slowly leaving your chest.

Rehearsal and application scenario:

Michelle was using derogatory words describing a group of students. When a student, Sherry, told Michelle her word choices were offensive, Michelle became defensive and would not take responsibility for her behavior.

Wrong way to respond? Right way to respond?

Student-created scenario:

Wrong way to respond? Right way to respond?

Targeted life skill: **SOCIAL AND CULTURAL AWARENESS**

Civility Academy

Definition: The ability to understand and appreciate one's personal social identity and cultural differences

Replacement behaviors:

Garden (different flowers all grow together)— Imagine you are helping maintain a garden. Plants in a garden, similar to people, grow and exist together. The soil represents the foundation of our world and our history. Every culture has its roots in the same soil, representing our shared human history and origins. Each seed represents a different culture, and like seeds, cultures have their unique characteristics. Just as plants need water and sunlight, cultures grow and thrive through exchange, understanding, and acceptance.

A garden requires regular care, and similarly, understanding and appreciating other cultures is an ongoing process. Just as gardens face threats from pests and weeds, cultures also face challenges. These might come in the form of stereotypes, biases, or misunderstandings. Reflect on these questions: How does your role in nurturing diversity and cultural understanding at your school or in your community resemble a gardener's responsibilities in tending to a diverse garden? Are your actions caring for or hurting our garden?

Fill in the blanks— Imagine yourself in a new, culturally diverse setting. This could be a foreign country, a cultural festival, or a social gathering with people from various backgrounds. Visualize observing people's interactions, traditions, or behaviors that are unfamiliar to you. Mentally note aspects that you do not understand or have incomplete information about. *These are the blanks you need to fill.*

Now, imagine asking respectful, open-ended questions to learn more about these unfamiliar aspects. Visualize listening actively and empathetically to the responses, showing genuine interest in learning. Imagine processing the new information, comparing it with your preconceived notions, and recognizing any biases or assumptions you might have had. Think about how this new understanding changes your perspective or enriches your knowledge of the culture or social setting.

Lastly, imagine how you would apply this new understanding in your interactions within this setting. Visualize yourself respecting cultural norms, using appropriate language, and showing empathy and understanding.

Now, articulate the blanks you identified and how you went about filling them in.

Rehearsal and application scenario:

Brendon is caught making fun of a student named Jaspeer in class who wears a turban. When asked by the teacher why he feels it necessary to make fun of Jaspeer's turban, Brendon says he is just joking with him.

Wrong way to respond? Right way to respond?

Student-created scenario:

Wrong way to respond? Right way to respond?

continued →

Targeted life skill: **COEXISTING**

Civility Academy

Definition: The ability to accept other people's ideas, beliefs, and perspectives that do not align with yours and to be in the same space at the same time peacefully

Replacement behaviors:

Agree to disagree—Think of a topic you feel passionate about (religion, politics, sports, and so on). Imagine that you are explaining why you love or feel passionately about this topic. Imagine a friend or person you are speaking to responds with a different opinion, explaining their own reasons with equal passion. Both points of view are valid.

Visualize and acknowledge the feelings you have when you hear a differing opinion. This might include surprise, confusion, defensiveness, or even curiosity. These feelings are natural. Instead of debating or trying to convince the other person, you can ask questions to genuinely understand their perspective. You might ask, "What experiences led you to feel this way?" or "Can you tell me more about why you think or feel that?" The key is for you to understand that it's OK to have differing opinions, and what's most important is the respect and understanding extended toward others.

Pieces of a jigsaw puzzle—Visualize the concept of coexisting using a jigsaw puzzle to illustrate how different pieces, each unique in shape and design, come together to form a complete picture. Imagine the uniqueness of each piece; see the unique shape, curves, and edges of a single jigsaw puzzle piece.

Just as every person is unique in beliefs, values, and backgrounds, every jigsaw piece is unique in its design. Imagine how we are all connected: each piece connects with others. Though they're different, they rely on each other to form a cohesive image. In life, we need to find ways to connect with others despite our differences.

Rehearsal and application scenario:

Jamie and Jeff used to be best friends until they got into a major disagreement. They no longer hang out with each other, but whenever they run into each other, they glare and make mean comments, making it difficult to be in the same location without some sort of negative interaction.

Wrong way to respond? Right way to respond?

Student-created scenario:

Wrong way to respond? Right way to respond?

Targeted life skill: **OPEN-MINDED**

Civility Academy

Definition: The ability to admit what you do not know and the willingness to learn about new ideas and points of view in the interest of demonstrating tolerance and acceptance

Replacement behaviors:

Two sides of a coin—There are two sides of a coin. Each side of the coin represents an opposite viewpoint of a specific topic. Instead of just looking at your side of the coin, force yourself to flip the coin in your mind and examine and consider the other side (the opposing viewpoint).

Three As (ask questions, avoid becoming defensive, accept change)—Use the three As by asking information-seeking questions, avoiding becoming mad if you do not agree, and accepting that it is OK if you and the other student have different points of view. Practice the three As in your head before using them in a situation.

Rehearsal and application scenario:

Jeffie and Patricia get into a heated disagreement in the middle of class over how they want to complete a group assignment. Neither of them are willing to consider a different point of view and are refusing to work together.

Wrong way to respond? Right way to respond?

Student-created scenario:

Wrong way to respond? Right way to respond?

continued →

Targeted life skill: **PERSPECTIVE TAKING**

Civility Academy

Definition: The ability to put oneself in someone else's position or situation while considering how their experiences have influenced them

Replacement behaviors:

Zoom out (beyond your perspective)—Imagine having the ability to zoom out on a situation or disagreement, similar to how you zoom out on your phone or computer screen to see more of the context and details of a picture. Do the same when you find yourself just looking at the situation or conflict from a narrow perspective.

Narrate it from another person's standpoint—Imagine a problem in a story in as vivid detail as you can: the situation, the people involved, their actions, and their emotions. Focus on your character, their words, their body language, and their actions. Retell (narrate) the incident from the point of view of your character; think about this character's feelings, thoughts, and motivations. Imagine how this behavior might feel, such as frustration, joy, or confusion.

Now, switch perspectives and explain what happened from the other person's point of view (narrate the story from their perspective). Mentally "become" this other character. Reflect on the same situation from this new point of view through the eyes of this other character, feeling their emotions and thinking about their thoughts. Notice the difference in perception, feeling, and reaction between the two characters.

How did it feel to see the situation from someone else's point of view? Are there any new understandings or insights? How does this change your vision of the original situation?

Rehearsal and application scenario:

Suzie is continuously getting into arguments with other students about her opinions. She has a hard time letting other students share their opinions, which makes it hard for her to establish healthy relationships with other students.

Wrong way to respond? Right way to respond?

Student-created scenario:

Wrong way to respond? Right way to respond?

Targeted life skill: COMPASSION

Civility Academy

Definition: The ability to understand and share the feelings of another who is having a difficult time and the desire to offer help and support, with a willingness to do something about it

Replacement behaviors:

Kind acts daily—Visualize your surroundings, the people you meet, and the things you do during your daily routine. As you reflect on your day, identify moments where you can show kindness. It can be a small act like smiling at someone, offering help, or giving a genuine compliment. Imagine yourself performing these acts of kindness.

For example, imagine helping a family member with a chore without being asked, sharing a snack with a friend at school, complimenting a classmate, offering to carry something for a teacher, or smiling and saying "Hello" to a neighbor. Imagine how your acts of kindness make others feel; notice a smile, a word of thanks, and any positive change in the other person's behavior.

Next, focus on how these acts of kindness make *you* feel. You should notice feelings of happiness, fulfillment, and a sense of connection with others.

Can you commit to performing at least one act of kindness each day? You can decide in the morning what it might be or let it happen unexpectedly.

Offer help—Visualize someone you know (or a fictional character) who might be facing a challenge or difficulty. Imagine a specific situation where this person is struggling. It could be a friend having trouble with homework, a family member feeling unwell, or a neighbor facing some trouble. Notice how the person might be feeling in this situation and try and feel these emotions yourself. Recognize the signs that this person needs help (such as looking sad, stressed, or overwhelmed). Think about different ways you could offer help in this scenario.

Choose one form of help you can offer, whether it's listening, doing something practical, or giving emotional support. Imagine yourself offering this help. What did you say? How does the other person respond? How does this make you feel? Do you feel happy, satisfied, more connected?

Understanding and responding to others' feelings is a crucial part of compassion. Think of a real situation where you could offer help in the coming days. What is a simple plan on how you might approach this real-world situation?

Rehearsal and application scenario:

Roger is constantly making negative comments to other students who do not agree with his ideas. His comments are hurtful and make other students feel bad, but Roger does not seem to care.

Wrong way to respond? Right way to respond?

Student-created scenario:

Wrong way to respond? Right way to respond?

Organizational Skills Academy Behavior Rehearsal Cards

Organizational Skills Academy is designed for students struggling with organizational skills impacting readiness to learn and work completion. See the eight targeted life skills that align with the Organizational Skills Academy along with the corresponding behavior rehearsal cards (see table 4.4 and figure 4.4).

TABLE 4.4: Organizational Skills Academy At-A-Glance

Behavior Academy	Eight Targeted Life Skills	Replacement Behaviors
Organizational Skills Academy	**Stress management:** The ability to recognize the source of one's own stressors (challenges, pressures, anxieties, demands) and respond in a healthy manner	Make a list Circle of control
	Preparedness: The ability to be ready with the materials and knowledge to actively engage in class	Morning self-checklist Use a planner (calendar items, due dates)
	Resourceful: The ability to identify and use a variety of resources, tools, and materials to effectively find solutions to challenges or problems	Think outside the box Resource bank
	Flexibility: The ability to adapt and shift between the tasks, changes, and demands of various situations	Have a plan B Rubber band
	Goal setting: The ability to set time-targeted objectives and determine an action plan and steps necessary to achieve them	Visualize target Win this day
	Prioritizing: The ability to identify and organize tasks and assignments by due dates, amount of time required, and urgency	Important versus urgent list Chunking
	Initiative: The ability to see what assignments and tasks need to be completed and independently get started without waiting to be told or constantly reminded	Action before motivation Talk back to your inner critic
	Self-management: The ability to effectively manage one's time, energy, and space	Time blocking Develop and follow productive routines

Targeted life skill: **STRESS MANAGEMENT**

Organizational Skills Academy

Definition: The ability to recognize the source of one's own stressors (challenges, pressures, anxieties, demands) and respond in a healthy manner

Replacement behaviors:

Make a list—Visualize a time when you felt overwhelmed and stressed. Picture the specific details that were contributing to your stress. Recognize how you felt in that situation. Were you feeling rushed, anxious, disorganized, or so on? Imagine a small shift in your mind; see yourself taking a moment to pause. Now, picture yourself physically taking out a notepad and pen or opening a note-taking app on your phone. Envision writing down all the tasks that are contributing to your stress. Each task is written down, one by one.

Making a list is a way to organize thoughts and reduce stress, and the act of writing it down can help in decluttering the mind. Once the list is complete, visualize organizing it. You might categorize items, prioritize them, or plan steps to address each point. As you do this, notice any change in your feelings; perhaps a sense of control or clarity.

Now, visualize yourself addressing each item on the list, marking them off one at a time. Focus on the feeling of accomplishment and relief as you see items being crossed off. Notice the reduction in stress and increase in confidence as the list gets shorter. Reflect on this overall experience and how it felt to organize and tackle your tasks in a systematic way through imagery.

Circle of control—The circle of control is a simple tool that helps distinguish between things we can control (inside the circle) and things we cannot control (outside the circle). Visualize a large circle in front of you. This is your circle of control. Think about the things that are currently causing you stress. These could be upcoming exams, peer relationships, family issues, and so on. As you name each stressor, imagine placing it either inside or outside the circle. If it's something you can control (like your study habits, your reaction to a situation, your decisions, or your attitude), it goes inside the circle. If it's something you can't control (like the beliefs or behavior of others, global events, the weather, or your past), it goes outside the circle. Focus your attention on the items inside the circle.

Now, imagine how you might positively influence or change these things. This could involve setting study goals, practicing relaxation techniques, or seeking help from a teacher or counselor. For the items outside the circle, visualize acknowledging these concerns but then gently releasing them. You might imagine a breeze blowing these worries away, or the items dissolving into the air, symbolizing the acceptance of what you cannot change. While you have control over some aspects of your life, accepting what you can't change is also a powerful tool for stress management. Focus your energy and thoughts on what is within your power to change.

Rehearsal and application scenario:

Joseph feels like he is drowning in his classes and does not know where to begin, so he decides to avoid the work, which is making him more stressed.

Wrong way to respond? Right way to respond?

Student-created scenario:

Wrong way to respond? Right way to respond?

FIGURE 4.4: Organizational Skills Academy behavior rehearsal cards.

continued →

Targeted life skill: **PREPAREDNESS**

Organizational Skills Academy

Definition: The ability to be ready with the materials and knowledge to actively engage in class

Replacement behaviors:

Morning self-checklist—A checklist is a tool that helps people remember and complete tasks effectively. For example, imagine a piece of paper with a list of all the things you need to do today, with little boxes next to each task. Think of a morning when you are getting ready for school. Picture yourself waking up, getting out of bed, and starting your day.

Now, imagine you have a checklist on your desk or table. It has all the things you need to do this morning before leaving for school. Mentally go through each task on the checklist. See yourself looking at the checklist, brushing your teeth, and then checking off the task. Feel the satisfaction of marking it done. As you mentally check off tasks, notice how you feel less rushed and more in control as you check off each task and you're not forgetting anything important. How did it feel to use a checklist in your mind? How can this tool help in real life? Now, create and use a real checklist. You can start with simple daily tasks and gradually incorporate more complex schedules.

Use a planner (calendar items, due dates)—Imagine holding a planner in your hands (a physical planner or a digital one on a device). Visually, these are some ways you would use it:

Morning routine: Visualize yourself sitting down in the morning and opening your planner. You should see the pages filled with your schedule, tasks, and goals for the day.

Detailing the day: Visualize noting down assignments, setting reminders for important tasks, and blocking out time for studying, breaks, and relaxing activities.

Checking and updating: See yourself regularly consulting the planner throughout the day, checking off completed tasks, and adjusting as needed.

Imagine the sense of control and calm that comes from knowing what needs to be done and by when. Feel the satisfaction of checking off completed tasks. Picture a sudden change in plans (maybe a last-minute assignment or a canceled activity) and visualize adjusting your planner accordingly, experiencing how it helps manage stress and keeps you organized.

Finally, imagine the end of the day, reviewing your planner. You should feel a sense of accomplishment for what you've completed and use the planner to prepare for the next day. Practice this mental imagery regularly, especially in the evenings or mornings, to reinforce the habit of using a planner.

Rehearsal and application scenario:

Jose often forgets to come to class without his books and materials, assignments completed, and so on. He keeps falling further behind.

Wrong way to respond? Right way to respond?

Student-created scenario:

Wrong way to respond? Right way to respond?

Targeted life skill: **RESOURCEFUL**

Organizational Skills Academy

Definition: The ability to identify and use a variety of resources, tools, and materials to effectively find solutions to challenges or problems

Replacement behaviors:

Think outside the box—Visualize a closed square box. Inside the box are common tools and ways to solve problems. Outside the box are additional methods and tools to help solve problems. The box represents the typical response, but if that response is not working for you, give yourself permission to think of other nontypical ways and resources that will help you.

Resource bank—Imagine a bank in your mind. Real banks are places where people store their financial resources (money). The bank helps people be resourceful, save for the future, invest in opportunities, and have a safety net for unpredictable times. Instead of a bank helping you with finances, imagine a bank full of resources for you to help you make decisions and support you when you need them. When you notice certain resources, people, supports, and so on, helping you, make sure to mentally log this information in one place (your resource bank) you can access when you need additional help.

Rehearsal and application scenario:

Ralph does not understand the assignments but he does not want to bother the teacher or ask questions about the assignments in front of the other students so he decides to get the failing grades instead.

Wrong way to respond? Right way to respond?

Student-created scenario:

Wrong way to respond? Right way to respond?

continued →

Targeted life skill: **FLEXIBILITY**

Organizational Skills Academy

Definition: The ability to adapt and shift between the tasks, changes, and demands of various situations

Replacement behaviors:

Have a plan B—Imagine being in a boat going down a river. Plan A is using a planned path to get to the destination. However, an obstacle may come in the way, such as a log blocking the plan A path. The log represents an unexpected challenge or obstacle. Plan B, instead of panicking and hitting the log, is to take the side, longer-stream route and still get to your destination. This represents the importance of being flexible when faced with obstacles. Have a plan B.

Rubber band—Imagine yourself as a rubber band in a situation. No matter how much you are stretched and pulled in different directions, you will return to your original state. Similarly, when we are flexible in our thinking and actions, we can adjust and adapt to different situations without breaking or feeling overwhelmed.

Rehearsal and application scenario:

Trey has a hard time working through changes or challenges. When his original plan is interrupted, he gives up.

Wrong way to respond? Right way to respond?

Student-created scenario:

Wrong way to respond? Right way to respond?

Targeted life skill: GOAL SETTING

Organizational Skills Academy

Definition: The ability to set time-targeted objectives and determine an action plan and steps necessary to achieve them

Replacement behaviors:

Visualize target—Imagine a classic archery target. The bullseye represents a specific goal. This could be anything from "completing a big project" to "passing a hard test." Imagine the outer circles around the target being smaller steps toward reaching your goal; for example, "keeping up with each of the project component due dates" or "completing homework and studying for the test." Imagine an arrow pointed at the target. The arrow represents all your effort and hard work. The more effort and hard work, the more the arrow lands on the bullseye (goal).

Win this day—Each day, imagine a win. A win is making progress or meeting goals set for yourself. Determine what you are going to do to work toward the goal each day. Imagine a goal you have, such as "bringing a grade up." When you make steps toward accomplishing that goal (for example, "met with a teacher to help with incomplete assignments" and "went to voluntary tutoring to help with some concepts"), celebrate that as a win. Even if you haven't accomplished the entire goal yet, celebrate the actions you took toward reaching the goal; win the day.

Rehearsal and application scenario:

Maria is constantly setting unrealistic, broad goals for herself with no action, and when she does not meet them, she becomes discouraged and does not see the goal through.

Wrong way to respond? Right way to respond?

Student-created scenario:

Wrong way to respond? Right way to respond?

continued →

Targeted life skill: **PRIORITIZING**

Organizational Skills Academy

Definition: The ability to identify and organize tasks and assignments by due dates, amount of time required, and urgency

Replacement behaviors:

Important versus urgent list—Imagine a list of two categories: important and urgent. Important items can be finished by the end of the week or later, but the urgent items will need to be completed within a day or two. This will help you identify and move over what time or task is going to come first (urgent) and require time and energy. Mentally moving items to these categories will help you prioritize what is going to come first.

Chunking—Imagine yourself splitting (dividing) larger amounts of an overwhelming assignment or task into smaller, more doable chunks. Group these tasks by subject, deadline, or difficulty. Imagine organizing each chunk further by urgency or significance. Within each chunk, there are items of different importance. Begin with the items with the highest importance. Implement this technique in your real-world daily or weekly planning, starting with simple tasks and gradually moving to more complex projects.

Rehearsal and application scenario:

Zack has a difficult time deciding how much time or resources each assignment needs. He tends to begin with one assignment, and then his time runs out or he is tired when it comes to some assignments that are due.

Wrong way to respond? Right way to respond?

Student-created scenario:

Wrong way to respond? Right way to respond?

Targeted life skill: **INITIATIVE**

Organizational Skills Academy

Definition: The ability to see what assignments and tasks need to be completed and independently get started without waiting to be told or constantly reminded

Replacement behaviors:

Action before motivation—Imagine a familiar setting where you often need to take initiative, such as a classroom, sports field, or even at home. Next, picture a specific task or challenge in this setting in your current state of inaction, like beginning homework, participating in a class discussion, or starting a workout. Visualize taking the first small step related to the task. For example, opening a book, raising your hand, or putting on your sports gear. As you visualized taking action, did you notice any shift in your feelings?

Taking the first step, even mentally, can reduce feeling overwhelmed and increase feelings of control and optimism. See yourself continuing with small, successive actions such as reading a page, speaking up in class, or beginning to jog. Notice how your feelings start to change after initiating the action; you might begin to feel more engaged or interested. See yourself gaining momentum, becoming more involved and motivated as you continue. Visualize completing the task and feeling a sense of accomplishment. Reflect on how taking action led to a change in your motivation and feelings.

Talk back to your inner critic—Imagine a small character sitting on your shoulder. This character represents your inner critic, constantly whispering doubts and negative thoughts. Everyone has this inner voice that can sometimes be overly critical or negative. Recall a recent time when you felt discouraged or doubtful. Imagine the inner critic speaking those discouraging words.

Now, imagine another character, this one representing your inner advocate or supporter. This character is kind, supportive, and always looks for the positive. Imagine a scenario where the inner critic starts to speak. Then, have the inner advocate step in and offer a positive, encouraging response. If the critic says, "Why even try when you'll probably fail?" the advocate might respond, "It's better to try and risk failure than to never try at all. Success comes from trying, learning, and persisting."

Here are some additional examples.

Inner Critic: "You always make mistakes."
Inner Advocate Response: "Mistakes are a part of learning. Every mistake is an opportunity to learn something new and improve."

Inner Critic: "No one likes you."
Inner Advocate Response: "You are valued and cared for. It's impossible to be liked by everyone, but there are people who appreciate and cherish you."

By using mental imagery in this structured way, you can develop a more positive inner dialogue and build resilience against self-doubt and negative thinking.

Rehearsal and application scenario:

Miriam gets overwhelmed when she sees all the assignments she has to complete. The teacher is constantly reminding her to get started on the work, but she feels numb and unable to begin.

Wrong way to respond? Right way to respond?

Student-created scenario:

Wrong way to respond? Right way to respond?

continued →

Targeted life skill: **SELF-MANAGEMENT**

Organizational Skills Academy

Definition: The ability to effectively manage one's time, energy, and space

Replacement behaviors:

Time blocking—Time blocking is a time-management method that involves dividing your day into blocks of time, each dedicated to accomplishing a specific task or group of tasks. Now, imagine your day from start to finish. Picture yourself waking up, going through your morning routine, and then beginning your school day or activities. As you visualize, mentally insert blocks of time for each main task you need or want to accomplish. In your mind's eye, assign different colors to how much time each task will take: red represents 2 hours or more, blue represents 1 hour, and green represents 30 minutes or less. For instance, schoolwork tasks might be red, personal errands could be blue, and leisure time might be green. This color-coding helps you quickly identify and organize how to block an appropriate amount of time for each task or activity in a visually appealing and structured way.

Imagine yourself completing a task, and then visualize a clear transition to the next one. This could be as simple as standing up, stretching, and then sitting back down to start a new task. This mental practice can help you prepare for the actual transitions during your day, making them smoother and more efficient. Imagine potential distractions or interruptions that could arise during your time blocks. Then, visualize yourself handling these interruptions effectively, perhaps by jotting down the distraction for later and refocusing on your current task.

At the end of your visualized day, imagine looking back over your time blocks. Which ones were successful? Did you assign the task an appropriate amount of time? Where did you struggle to stay on task? Use these reflections to adjust your approach for the next day.

Develop and follow productive routines—Walk through your daily routines in your head, write them down, and follow them consistently. Begin with one or two routines: "I will work on assignments and tasks every day from 4:00–5:00 p.m. after I get home from school without technology distractions" or "Every Monday, Wednesday, and Friday, I will work in a quiet spot in the library after school until the late bus arrives."

Rehearsal and application scenario:

Ray is easily distracted with other preferred activities in place of the assignments or tasks he has to complete.

Wrong way to respond? Right way to respond?

Student-created scenario:

Wrong way to respond? Right way to respond?

Social Skills Academy Behavior Rehearsal Cards

Social Skills Academy is designed for students struggling with appropriate peer and adult interactions. See the eight targeted life skills that align with Social Skills Academy along with the corresponding behavior rehearsal cards (see table 4.5 and figure 4.5, page 96).

TABLE 4.5: Social Skills Academy At-A-Glance

Behavior Academy	Eight Targeted Life Skills	Replacement Behaviors
Social Skills Academy	**Social awareness:** The ability to notice, understand, and respond to social cues, unwritten rules, and social interactions, and respond to them appropriately	Social radar Social translator
	Self-awareness: The ability to recognize and understand your own thoughts, feelings, perspectives, strengths, weaknesses, and motivations and how you react to a variety of situations	Magic mirror Study your character's story
	Turn taking: The ability to understand when it is your turn to speak, answer a question, participate, and interact in a game, and when it is appropriate to give someone else a chance to do the same	Game of catch Invisible microphone
	Empathy: The ability to put yourself in someone else's position, attempting to understand and imagine how you would feel or think if you were in their situation and how you can respond in a caring way	Superpower to understand other people's feelings Put yourself in someone else's shoes
	Cooperation: The ability to work together while sharing resources and being willing to compromise to get to a common goal	Imagine a team game (role or job) Step out of your comfort zone (try something new each day)
	Relationship building: The ability to make and maintain meaningful, healthy connections with others	Practice chats or short conversations Building a bridge
	Communication (verbal and nonverbal): The ability to actively listen and use both verbal (using words) and nonverbal (body language, facial expressions, gestures) methods to express thoughts and feelings in a positive manner	Visible bubble Give one or two compliments a day
	Patience: The ability to wait calmly without getting upset or angry, even if you want something right away	Picture the positive outcome for waiting Distraction

Targeted life skill: SOCIAL AWARENESS

Social Skills Academy

Definition: The ability to notice, understand, and respond to social cues, unwritten rules, and social interactions, and respond to them appropriately

Replacement behaviors:

Social radar—Imagine a radar. A typical radar helps detect items (airplane, ship, and so on) and sends signals of how far they are, how fast they are going, and so on. Imagine having a radar for social interactions. When in a social situation, remember to turn on your "social radar" by noticing other students around you, what they are doing, how they are interacting, and so on. Use this information to help you interact with them.

Social translator—A translator takes something that is written or said and says it in a different language for others to understand. Imagine being a social translator. Translate the behaviors you are seeing in a social situation in your own words, similar to someone who can translate another language. Imagine a classroom setting where two students are having a disagreement about a group project. Describe their body language, tone of voice, and facial expressions. One student might be crossing their arms and speaking loudly, while the other avoids eye contact and speaks softly. Interpret these cues and think about how a social translator might help mediate the situation.

Visualize a lunchroom scene where a new student is sitting alone while others are in groups. Focus on the new student's body language, the dynamics among other students, and the overall atmosphere of the room. How might a social translator recognize feelings of exclusion and think of ways to promote inclusivity?

Picture a student receiving feedback on a project in front of the class. Describe the student's reaction to both positive and negative feedback, noting changes in facial expression, posture, and engagement. Analyze the different emotional responses; how could a social translator support or encourage the student?

Rehearsal and application scenario:

Martin wants to join a game, so he walks into an existing game and grabs the ball from another student. The students in the game become upset and tell him to get out of the game.

Wrong way to respond? Right way to respond?

Student-created scenario:

Wrong way to respond? Right way to respond?

Targeted life skill: SELF-AWARENESS

Social Skills Academy

Definition: The ability to recognize and understand your own thoughts, feelings, perspectives, strengths, weaknesses, and motivations and how you react to a variety of situations

Replacement behaviors:

Magic mirror—Imagine you are looking into a magic mirror that helps you see and understand what you are thinking and feeling in situations with friends and so on. Ask your magic mirror (yourself) to help you be more aware of your social interactions. What does the mirror show about how you react when you're frustrated?

Study your character's story—Imagine yourself as the main character in your life story. Study yourself as a character in this story and identify traits, behaviors, and emotions of your character. Focus on how your character typically reacts to different events, such as success, failure, stress, or happiness. Recognize patterns in your character's behavior, and ask the following questions.

- What did you learn about your character?

- How does your character respond to challenges?

- What are your character's strengths and weaknesses?

Rehearsal and application scenario:

Ralyn is constantly seeking the attention of other students. In her desire to be accepted, she is easily convinced to be involved in scenarios that do not concern her.

Wrong way to respond? Right way to respond?

Student-created scenario:

Wrong way to respond? Right way to respond?

FIGURE 4.5: Social Skills Academy behavior rehearsal cards.

continued →

Targeted life skill: **TURN TAKING**

Social Skills Academy

Definition: The ability to understand when it is your turn to speak, answer a question, participate, and interact in a game, and when it is appropriate to give someone else a chance to do the same

Replacement behaviors:

Game of catch—Imagine a game of catch. Each person has to wait their turn to throw and catch the ball. The same exists when you are having a conversation with someone. Practice letting each person have a chance to speak before you speak or interact.

Invisible microphone—Microphones are used for when it is someone's turn to speak, sing, and so on. Imagine an invisible microphone in your hand when you are having a conversation or interaction. The microphone is on for the person who is speaking. Wait until your microphone is on (your turn to speak).

Rehearsal and application scenario:

Robyn interrupts constantly when someone is trying to have a conversation with him. He also only engages in whatever activity he wants to engage in without the compromise of trying something someone else wants to do.

Wrong way to respond? Right way to respond?

Student-created scenario:

Wrong way to respond? Right way to respond?

Targeted life skill: **EMPATHY**

Social Skills Academy

Definition: The ability to put yourself in someone else's position, attempting to understand and imagine how you would feel or think if you were in their situation and how you can respond in a caring way

Replacement behaviors:

Superpower to understand other people's feelings—Superheroes have special powers. Imagine you have a special superhero power to help you understand other people's feelings—the power to connect with people's hearts and minds. Turn on the superhero power to help remind you to notice other people's feelings in different situations. Visualize a scenario involving a peer or a fictional character who is facing a difficult situation. It could be someone dealing with a challenge at school, at home, or in a social setting. Use your powers to imagine yourself in the shoes of that person.

Notice the surroundings, the expressions on the faces of people involved, and the body language. Tune into the emotions that person might be feeling (sadness, frustration, anxiety, or something else). How did this exercise help you to connect with the feelings of others?

Understanding emotions is like using a superpower to connect with and support others.

Put yourself in someone else's shoes—Think of a common experience like feeling left out, struggling with a task, or facing a challenge. Now, visualize yourself in the chosen scenario. Imagine you are the new kid in school. You're sitting alone at lunch because you haven't made friends yet. How do you feel? Are you feeling lonely, scared, or maybe hopeful that someone will join you?

How would you want others to treat you in that situation? What could someone do to make you feel better? A smile, an invitation to sit with them, a kind word?

Look for opportunities to show empathy to others using this new understanding. Next time you see someone sitting alone, remember this feeling. What can you do to help?

Rehearsal and application scenario:

Larry is constantly in the center of drama between groups of students. He gossips constantly and shares hurtful information with each group to cause problems.

Wrong way to respond? Right way to respond?

Student-created scenario:

Wrong way to respond? Right way to respond?

continued →

Targeted life skill: **COOPERATION**

Social Skills Academy

Definition: The ability to work together while sharing resources and being willing to compromise to get to a common goal

Replacement behaviors:

Imagine a team game (role or job)—Imagine a team game or project. Identify what everyone is trying to accomplish. What is the goal? Identify everyone's role or job in the game or project (including your own) toward achieving the goal. Each role, no matter how small it seems, is crucial for the success of the whole group.

Think of a challenge that the team must overcome, then describe how each team member contributes to addressing this challenge. Describe how, through cooperation and everyone playing their part, the team overcomes the challenge. Highlight moments of teamwork, such as players assisting each other in scoring or scientists combining their expertise to solve a problem. Reflect on how success was achieved not by any single member but by everyone working together. Each role, when performed well and in coordination with others, contributed to the achievement.

Step out of your comfort zone (try something new each day)—A comfort zone is a safe place (mentally or physically) where a person is not tested or asked to do something the person does not usually do. Inside a comfort zone, people will not typically like to experience new things. They will only do what is comfortable or familiar. Take it one step at a time to try at least one new thing a day (for example, say "Hi" to someone you may normally just walk past, ask to join an activity or game you would normally avoid, and so on).

Rehearsal and application scenario:

Lilly struggles to work well with other students during group assignments because it makes her uncomfortable. She asks the teacher if she can work alone instead.

Wrong way to respond? Right way to respond?

Student-created scenario:

Wrong way to respond? Right way to respond?

Targeted life skill: RELATIONSHIP BUILDING

Social Skills Academy

Definition: The ability to make and maintain meaningful, healthy connections with others

Replacement behaviors:

Practice chats or short conversations—Imagine yourself having a short chat or conversation with a person. Think about and plan one or two things you are going to say or talk about (say "Hi" or ask a question). When possible, start, engage, and practice one or two short chats or short conversations a day with someone. While questions are a great way to initiate conversation, remember that the quality of conversation and depth of connection will rely more on your general interest and active listening than on the specific questions you ask.

Building a bridge—Imagine that you see two islands separated by water. These are people. In order for these two islands (people) to connect, they need a bridge. The bridge represents the efforts and actions we take to build and maintain relationships.

Imagine laying a solid foundation on both sides of the water. This foundation is important for the stability of the bridge. In relationships, it represents establishing trust and respect. Then, visualize the supports or pillars rising from the foundation. These are important to hold the bridge. These supports represent ongoing communication and efforts to understand each other. Now, see the deck being laid across the supports, creating the path across. This deck is like the shared experiences, values, and interests that create a path for a deeper connection. Imagine adding handrails and safety features to the bridge. In relationships, these are like setting healthy boundaries and supporting one another.

Once the bridge is built, visualize you and the other person meeting in the middle of the bridge. This meeting point symbolizes the ongoing nurturing of the relationship, where each person makes an effort to come halfway. Just as a real bridge needs frequent maintenance, so do relationships. Imagine regular checks and repairs on the bridge, reflecting the need for continuous effort in a relationship. How can this metaphor of building and maintaining a bridge be applied in real-life relationships?

Rehearsal and application scenario:

Farah tries to hang out with other students, but even though she stands near them during break, they do not interact with her. She also does not know what to say, so she awkwardly stands there without saying anything to them.

Wrong way to respond? Right way to respond?

Student-created scenario:

Wrong way to respond? Right way to respond?

continued →

Targeted life skill: **COMMUNICATION** (verbal and nonverbal)

Social Skills Academy

Definition: The ability to actively listen and use both verbal (using words) and nonverbal (body language, facial expressions, gestures) methods to express thoughts and feelings in a positive manner

Replacement behaviors:

Visible bubble—The visible bubble represents an imaginary bubble that surrounds each person, symbolizing your personal space, comfort zone, and the area where effective communication occurs. Visualize yourself in a comfortable space and imagine a bubble forming around you. This bubble is flexible and changes size based on your communication and comfort levels. The size of the bubble might change in different scenarios. For example, the bubble might be larger in unfamiliar settings or with strangers, indicating a need for more personal space. With friends and family, the bubble might shrink, reflecting comfort and openness to closer communication. The bubble can help in understanding nonverbal cues. If someone steps back, their bubble is expanding, possibly indicating discomfort or a need for more space. If they lean in, their bubble is shrinking, showing interest and engagement.

Adjust your communication style according to the perceived size and nature of the other person's bubble.

Give one or two compliments a day—Imagine how it feels when someone gives you a compliment (someone says you are good at playing a sport, you always listen to someone in need, and so on). Practice thinking about possible compliments you can give to someone. Compliments need to be specific, sincere, and not overused. For example, you can give compliments about someone's personal qualities, skills, or work ethic.

Some examples include: "I have always appreciated how kind you are," "I like your shirt," and "You always have a positive attitude." Give one or two compliments a day in a positive manner, similar to the samples provided, while being specific and sincere.

Rehearsal and application scenario:

Steven makes inappropriate comments to get attention from other students.

Wrong way to respond? Right way to respond?

Student-created scenario:

Wrong way to respond? Right way to respond?

Targeted life skill: PATIENCE

Social Skills Academy

Definition: The ability to wait calmly without getting upset or angry, even if you want something right away

Replacement behaviors:

Picture the positive outcome for waiting— Picture yourself feeling good or achieving your outcome to help you see why it is worth the wait. For example, if it is difficult to wait for your turn at a game. While you are waiting, imagine what you are going to do when you are in the game and how good it is going to feel. Remind yourself of the great outcome you'll experience for waiting.

Distraction—A distraction is something that happens that moves your attention from one thing to something else (noise, another activity, and so on). A distraction can also help make waiting for something you want to do or get right away seem shorter and help you with patience. When you are feeling impatient, imagine a distraction (something else you can do during the waiting time, such as start a new game, talk to someone, read a book, and so on), and do it in the meantime.

Rehearsal and application scenario:

Vang struggles when waiting for his turn and gets upset and begins to scream at other students if he thinks they are taking too long. The other students do not like playing with Vang when he gets this way.

Wrong way to respond? Right way to respond?

Student-created scenario:

Wrong way to respond? Right way to respond?

Upstander Academy Behavior Rehearsal Cards

Upstander Academy is designed for students demonstrating or participating in bullying-type behaviors. See the eight targeted life skills that align with Upstander Academy along with the corresponding behavior rehearsal cards (see table 4.6 and figure 4.6).

TABLE 4.6: Upstander Academy At-A-Glance

Behavior Academy	Eight Targeted Life Skills	Replacement Behaviors
Upstander Academy	**Self-perception:** The ability to identify how you see yourself and how this impacts your behaviors, feelings, relationships, and decisions	Glasses (lens) Self-compliment a day (be nice to yourself)
	Empathy: The ability to put yourself in someone else's position and attempt to understand and imagine how you would feel or think if you were in the situation and how you can respond in a caring way	Recognize and name someone else's emotions Empathy map
	Action oriented: The ability to see a problem, then plan and take the next steps to create solutions	Superhero saving the world Shut it down (turn off switch)
	Analyzing situations: The ability to take a problem or situation and dissect it into smaller parts in a nonjudgmental way to understand how all the parts impact the problem, interaction, or relationships	Step out of your body Decision tree
	Self-confidence: The ability to positively believe in one's own ability, skills, and worth when it comes to accomplishing tasks and improving social interactions	Daily positive affirmations Self-mantra tagline
	Digital citizenship: The ability to understand and use online technology in a responsible and positive way while communicating or sharing information	Parent or guardian rule Digital footprint
	Moral leadership: The ability and courage to follow your values and do the right thing even when others are not	Captain of your own ship Moral compass
	Problem solving: The ability to understand a problem and break down the possible solutions into smaller steps and actions	Solution to every problem mindset Pros and cons

Targeted life skill: SELF-PERCEPTION

Upstander Academy

Definition: The ability to identify how you see yourself and how this impacts your behaviors, feelings, relationships, and decisions

Replacement behaviors:

Glasses (lens)—Glasses are often worn to aid vision, correct vision, protect from the light, and so on. Imagine you have glasses that you can wear to aid your focus with how you see your own behaviors and actions to help you self-correct on the spot.

Self-compliment a day (be nice to yourself)—A compliment is praise or admiration you give someone that helps the person receiving it feel good about themself. Imagine a compliment you can give yourself and how that would make you feel. Give yourself at least one compliment a day ("I am a good person," "I am good at helping others," and so on). For every negative thing you catch your inner voice saying to yourself, counter it with a compliment.

Rehearsal and application scenario:

Sara compares herself to who she believes are the "popular girls" in her class. She wishes she could be like them and in their group, but she never feels welcome.

Wrong way to respond? Right way to respond?

Student-created scenario:

Wrong way to respond? Right way to respond?

FIGURE 4.6: Upstander Academy behavior rehearsal cards. continued →

Targeted life skill: **EMPATHY**

Upstander Academy

Definition: The ability to put yourself in someone else's position and attempt to understand and imagine how you would feel or think if you were in the situation and how you can respond in a caring way

Replacement behaviors:

Recognize and name someone else's emotions—It is important to recognize your own emotions; however, it is also important to understand the emotions of others. Their emotions may be similar to or different from yours. Take a minute to put your feelings aside; then imagine, recognize, and name someone else's emotions in a scenario or current situation you are experiencing with another person.

Empathy map—A map presents information in a visual format about locations, landmarks, physical terrain, distances, and so on. Landmarks help us recognize and locate specific points on a map. Imagine someone going through a challenging time or situation. Map out these "emotional landmarks" (empathy map) you think the person is experiencing (sad, embarrassed, lonely, angry, and so on) and why. This will help you empathize with the person's emotional journey of feelings beyond your own.

Rehearsal and application scenario:

Kei joins in when he sees his friend Stephan making fun of students. He laughs and adds to the comments even though the other students look visibly upset and have asked them to stop.

Wrong way to respond? Right way to respond?

Student-created scenario:

Wrong way to respond? Right way to respond?

Targeted life skill: **ACTION ORIENTED**

Upstander Academy

Definition: The ability to see a problem, then plan and take the next steps to create solutions

Replacement behaviors:

Superhero saving the world—A superhero is known for seeing problems and helping solve them before they become larger. Imagine yourself as a superhero. Ask yourself, "What would a superhero do in this situation?" If you see a problem beginning, find your inner superhero and work on a solution instead of stirring the pot or adding to the problem. A superhero does not always work alone. All superheroes have people they trust to help them when needed. For example, you can help stop a situation from getting bigger (escalating) by asking for help from a friend or adult.

Shut it down (turn off switch)—Imagine turning off a switch when you see a problem you can shut down in an instant instead of letting it become bigger (for example, spreading rumors). The switch represents your actions in the scenario.

Rehearsal and application scenario:

Lesly knows there's something stirring up between two students who like the same person, but instead of helping stop the scenario, she instigates the problem between the two students.

Wrong way to respond? Right way to respond?

Student-created scenario:

Wrong way to respond? Right way to respond?

continued →

Targeted life skill: ANALYZING SITUATIONS

Upstander Academy

Definition: The ability to take a problem or situation and dissect it into smaller parts in a nonjudgmental way to understand how all the parts impact the problem, interaction, or relationships

Replacement behaviors:

Step out of your body—Take a minute to imagine stepping out of your body (mentally distancing yourself from your immediate emotions or reactions) to watch and analyze the situation as an outsider would. Try to see yourself, others involved, and the surroundings. What do you observe about yourself, your reactions, your body language, your emotions, and your choices? How are others reacting? This will help you gain an objective perspective on situations by mentally distancing yourself from your immediate emotions and reactions.

Decision tree—Imagine a tree with its trunk, branches, and leaves. The trunk will represent the main problem or decision that needs to be made. The branches are possible paths or options, and the leaves are the potential benefits and obstacles. Use a decision tree strategy to analyze or walk yourself through a tough situation.

Rehearsal and application scenario:

Francine follows along with her group when the others decide they do not like someone. She is the one who will confront other students in front of everyone and try to embarrass them when she is around her group.

Wrong way to respond? Right way to respond?

Student-created scenario:

Wrong way to respond? Right way to respond?

Targeted life skill: **SELF-CONFIDENCE**

Upstander Academy

Definition: The ability to positively believe in one's own ability, skills, and worth when it comes to accomplishing tasks and improving social interactions

Replacement behaviors:

Daily positive affirmations—Positive affirmations are used to counter negative thoughts about yourself. Think about those negative thoughts that hurt your self-confidence. For example, if you find yourself comparing yourself to others and feeling bad, upset, or even jealous, with comments such as, "I am not as good as him" or "I will never have as many friends as her," flip your thinking to say two or three positive affirmations to yourself on a daily basis instead. Some examples include "I can do it," "I am a kind person and a good friend," "I can do hard things," "I am capable of overcoming this," or "I will get through this."

Self-mantra tagline—A mantra tagline is a short statement to help capture what a company or person is trying to project about themselves. For example, companies like Apple, Nike, and Disney use mantra taglines such as Apple's "Think different," Nike's "Just do it," and Disney's "The happiest place on earth" as their mantra taglines. Imagine your own self-mantra tagline that will help you with your self-confidence that you can say to yourself and reference it often to help you. Some examples could be, "Be your best self," or "I embrace challenges with courage and grace."

Rehearsal and application scenario:

Madison is jealous of Iliana because Iliana is now best friends with Madison's old best friend. Madison feels so bad inside about this that she develops a dislike for Iliana, writes things about her in the restrooms, and spreads rumors about her.

Wrong way to respond? Right way to respond?

Student-created scenario:

Wrong way to respond? Right way to respond?

continued →

Targeted life skill: **DIGITAL CITIZENSHIP**

Upstander Academy

Definition: The ability to understand and use online technology in a responsible and positive way while communicating or sharing information

Replacement behaviors:

Parent or guardian rule—Imagine a parent or guardian next to you before making a decision. Ask yourself, "Would I act this way if a parent or guardian was next to me watching?" For example, before posting something on social media, or saying something hurtful about a person that can ruin their reputation, would you do that if your parent or guardian was next to you? This will help remind you of what is appropriate.

Digital footprint—A footprint is the impression left on a surface from a shoe. Similar to a shoe footprint, imagine a digital footprint that does not go away while using technology. Remind yourself whatever you put in social media can be traced back to your digital footprint and stop typing or posting. Deleting does not mean the digital footprint is erased, so keep that in mind and make good choices.

Rehearsal and application scenario:

Jasper created an anonymous account to bully other students in his grade level. He shares embarrassing secrets and pictures through this avenue and believes no one will find out because it is anonymous.

Wrong way to respond? Right way to respond?

Student-created scenario:

Wrong way to respond? Right way to respond?

Targeted life skill: **MORAL LEADERSHIP**

Upstander Academy

Definition: The ability and courage to follow your values and do the right thing even when others are not

Replacement behaviors:

Captain of your own ship—The responsibility of a captain includes steering the ship in the right direction toward a destination while keeping all passengers or cargo safe. Imagine yourself as the captain of your own ship (your life scenarios) and being able to steer (move) the ship toward the right direction through your actions and leadership. Make choices as the captain of your life.

Moral compass—A compass is an instrument that helps give people directions. Imagine having a moral compass that can help guide your actions (the direction you are taking) and help you see if this is the right or wrong direction or if this direction is going to hurt others. Pull out your imaginary "inner moral compass" when having to make difficult decisions.

Rehearsal and application scenario:

Luke is a nice student but tends to find himself with a group of students who pick on other students. More than anything, they just exclude other students and make them feel like they do not belong.

Wrong way to respond? Right way to respond?

Student-created scenario:

Wrong way to respond? Right way to respond?

continued →

Targeted life skill: **PROBLEM SOLVING**

Upstander Academy

Definition: The ability to understand a problem and break down the possible solutions into smaller steps and actions

Replacement behaviors:

Solution to every problem mindset—A mindset is how people make sense of what is going on around them and how they decide to respond. When you find yourself in a tough and overwhelming situation (problem) or having a mindset that no solutions exist, assure yourself by practicing having a "there is a solution to every problem" mindset. When you have a problem, tell yourself there is a solution to every problem and imagine the possible solutions. One way you can imagine the possible solutions to a problem using this mindset is: accept it, change it, or leave it. If you cannot accept how something is going (the problem), then commit to making some changes by doing something different to try to solve it. If you can't change the situation (problem), remove yourself in any way and begin moving forward, which in some cases is the best solution. Having the mindset that there is a solution to every problem will help you stay focused on solving the problem.

Pros and cons—Use pros and cons to help you break down your possible solutions to a problem. Pros represent the advantages that go with a solution you have in mind, and cons represent the disadvantages of a solution you have in mind. For example, a solution to a problem may be enlisting the help of an adult on campus. The pros could be helping someone out by telling an adult and stopping the problem from getting bigger, but the cons may be getting caught between two friends or someone blaming you for getting them in trouble. Looking at both the pros and cons will help you decide what is the better action to help solve the problem.

Rehearsal and application scenario:

When Diana feels upset, she thinks that the only way for her to feel better is to teach the student who upset her a lesson by getting revenge.

Wrong way to respond? Right way to respond?

Student-created scenario:

Wrong way to respond? Right way to respond?

Visit **go.SolutionTree.com/behavior/BA** *for a free reproducible version of this figure.*

Motivation Academy Behavior Rehearsal Cards

Motivation Academy is designed for students who appear apathetic toward incomplete work, grades, or being in class on time. See the eight targeted life skills that align with Motivation Academy along with the corresponding behavior rehearsal cards (see table 4.7 and figure 4.7, page 114).

TABLE 4.7: Motivation Academy At-A-Glance

Behavior Academy	Eight Targeted Life Skills	Replacement Behaviors
Motivation Academy	**Self-efficacy:** The ability to believe in yourself and your ability to complete tasks or accomplish goals	Evidence you can do it (use proof) Daily positive affirmations
	Growth mindset: The ability to believe you can learn and accomplish new things	Safe parking space Positive self-talk
	Self-monitoring: The ability to pay close attention, observe, and keep track of what works for you to improve behaviors and actions	Self-observations and self-grade Celebrate small wins
	Punctuality: The ability to be aware and on time to class, complete assignments by set timelines, follow schedules, and respect others' time and commitments	Set alarm clock Behavior streak
	Dependable: The ability to consistently follow through in a reliable way on what you told yourself or others you would do	Take a job or responsibility Create and follow a schedule
	Self-advocacy: The ability to understand your needs and rights and communicate them to others in a respectful way when they are not met	Assertive communication Speak up
	Goal setting: The ability to set time-targeted objectives and determine an action plan and the steps necessary to achieve them	Visualize goal and action plan Goal signposts
	Self-concept: The ability to understand perceptions and beliefs about oneself (positive or negative)	Challenge negative self-thoughts Self-portrait (strengths and weaknesses)

Targeted life skill: **SELF-EFFICACY**

Motivation Academy

Definition: The ability to believe in yourself and your ability to complete tasks or accomplish goals

Replacement behaviors:

Evidence you can do it (use proof)—Evidence are facts or information to help prove something. Use this same thinking about evidence to help you believe you can accomplish a goal or task.

Imagine some other times you did not believe in yourself at first, but persevering helped you to accomplish something. When you are feeling like you can't do something, imagine those times from the past and use that as evidence (proof) you can do it and to challenge your negative thoughts.

Daily positive affirmations—Positive affirmations are used to counter negative thoughts about yourself. Think about those negative thoughts telling you that you cannot do it. For example, "It is not worth it; I can't do it" or "I will never get this done; it is too hard."

Flip your thinking to say two or three positive affirmations to yourself on a daily basis instead. Some examples include "I can do it," "I can do hard things," "I am capable of overcoming this," and "I will get through this."

Rehearsal and application scenario:

Turner does not believe he is capable of performing at high levels in class and completing all his assignments in class. Instead of trying, Turner feels as if it is pointless.

Wrong way to respond? Right way to respond?

Student-created scenario:

Wrong way to respond? Right way to respond?

Targeted life skill: **GROWTH MINDSET**

Motivation Academy

Definition: The ability to believe you can learn and accomplish new things

Replacement behaviors:

Safe parking space—A parking space is a closed or open spot to park a car safely. Imagine a safe parking spot in your head where you are allowed to make mistakes and not fear them; a place where you feel entirely safe, supported, and at peace. In this space, there are no "failures," only learning experiences. Visualize any misstep or mistake as a learning opportunity. Give yourself permission to park in your safe parking spot whenever you need help to continue working toward your goal or task.

Positive self-talk—Positive self-talk is something you can do to encourage and motivate yourself to look at the bright side. Use positive self-talk to keep you going when things get tough or when you feel overwhelmed. For example, "Even if I am behind, it doesn't mean I cannot catch up if I break things down and start with one thing at a time" or "I haven't finished yet, but if I keep going, I will soon."

Rehearsal and application scenario:

Jack was once called out by a teacher for answering a question incorrectly in front of the class. Since that day, he feels like he is stupid and refuses to participate in class.

Wrong way to respond? Right way to respond?

Student-created scenario:

Wrong way to respond? Right way to respond?

FIGURE 4.7: Motivation Academy behavior rehearsal cards.

continued →

Targeted life skill: SELF-MONITORING

Motivation Academy

Definition: The ability to pay close attention, observe, and keep track of what works for you to improve behaviors and actions

Replacement behaviors:

Self-observations and self-grade—Observing requires someone to notice or see something they think may be important. Imagine being asked to observe and grade yourself. You are observing and grading yourself on effort and quality. Identify what grade you would give yourself based on your observation. How will you continue to improve on that grade by changing behaviors you observed not to be helpful?

Celebrate small wins—A small win is achieving a smaller goal or outcome you set for yourself. A small win may not seem important but when you self-monitor small wins, they begin to add up to bigger wins and motivate you to keep going. By visualizing these small wins, you can create a positive feedback loop. Visualization isn't just about seeing; it's about feeling the emotions tied to the success. When a goal or task is overwhelming, imagine some small wins toward the goal or completion of the task. Throughout each day, stop and celebrate the small wins you were monitoring by sharing with yourself, a friend, a teacher, or a family member. There will be days without obvious small wins or setbacks. On such days, it is essential to remind yourself to visualize the larger picture and the value of persistence. Every day might not be a win, but not giving up is a small win in itself.

Rehearsal and application scenario:

Dara is not consistent with her classroom performance. Sometimes she is on track, and other times she finds herself overwhelmed and behind. This makes Dara want to quit completely.

Wrong way to respond? Right way to respond?

Student-created scenario:

Wrong way to respond? Right way to respond?

Targeted life skill: PUNCTUALITY

Motivation Academy

Definition: The ability to be aware and on time to class, complete assignments by set timelines, follow schedules, and respect others' time and commitments

Replacement behaviors:

Set alarm clock—An alarm clock helps alert people of a specific time. People use alarm clocks to help them wake up, be on time to events and commitments, and turn in things on time. Being punctual is about respecting your commitment to a particular time. Imagine an alarm clock in your head (you can also set a concrete alarm clock on your phone or device, but it should be impossible to ignore).

Visualize yourself springing into action immediately upon hearing the alarm. This can be getting up from bed, leaving for school on time, or turning an assignment in when due. Now, link this immediate action to the positive feelings and results of being punctual—respect from peers, a sense of accomplishment, reduced stress, and so on.

Contrast the consequences of ignoring the alarm: feelings of guilt, others waiting, missed opportunities, and so on. This contrast can make this positive visualization even more powerful.

Behavior streak—A streak helps you keep track of how many days you have engaged in or met a goal toward a new positive behavior. It is motivating to want to keep your positive streak going. Set a goal (that is, being to class on time consistently even when you are not motivated to go, or turn in all assignments on time this week) and follow your streak.

Rehearsal and application scenario:

Arthur finds himself late to class daily. When he hears the bell ring, instead of walking straight to class, he decides to use the bathroom and even catch up with a few more friends who are also late to class. When he does get to class, Arthur appears to the teacher as if he does not care that he is late.

Wrong way to respond? Right way to respond?

Student-created scenario:

Wrong way to respond? Right way to respond?

continued →

Targeted life skill: **DEPENDABLE**

Motivation Academy

Definition: The ability to consistently follow through in a reliable way on what you told yourself or others you would do

Replacement behaviors:

Take a job or responsibility—Imagine an adult who has a full-time job. The adult is required to report to work on time and is responsible for various job requirements. Encourage yourself to take a job or responsibility at school or in class and be consistent. Whenever you do not want to do the job or follow through on your responsibility, imagine an adult in the workplace.

By drawing these parallels between school and work and emphasizing the value of dependability in both settings, you can gain a better understanding of the real-world importance of being reliable and responsible.

Create and follow a schedule—Create and follow a consistent schedule that works for you to help keep you on track every day. Mentally visualize your day from morning to night. Think about your routines, the tasks you need to complete, and the commitments you need to honor. Now, visualize a planner or digital calendar that lists all your tasks, appointments, and commitments for the day. You may also emphasize color coding for different activities, such as different classes or subjects; personal items, such as chores at home; or recreational activities, such as music lessons or sports practice.

Then, visualize the positive outcomes of following the schedule. You're on time for class, you complete assignments efficiently and teachers praise your punctuality, you have free time because you were efficient, and you feel a sense of accomplishment at the end of the day.

Rehearsal and application scenario:

Raja struggles to finish his part in group projects or complete his assignments. He tends to take a back-seat role in any projects or assignments due.

Wrong way to respond? Right way to respond?

Student-created scenario:

Wrong way to respond? Right way to respond?

Targeted life skill: SELF-ADVOCACY

Motivation Academy

Definition: The ability to understand your needs and rights and communicate them to others in a respectful way when they are not met

Replacement behaviors:

Assertive communication—Assertive communication is getting your point across in a direct but respectful way. In a situation where you think you need to advocate for yourself, imagine yourself telling the other person or asking the other person about something you need or feel "I need

_____

to help me complete this task" or "I feel

_____

when the work keeps piling up." Do not wait until you are completely unmotivated before trying to ask for help.

Speak up—Imagine a scenario where you are feeling unmotivated. This could be a classroom setting where you are struggling to focus on an assignment that feels too challenging or uninteresting. Perhaps you don't understand the assignment or feel it is too difficult given your current state of mind. The challenge is the inner voice telling you it's not worth the effort to ask for help or clarification. You understand that advocating for yourself is necessary, despite the lack of motivation. You remind yourself of the importance of your needs and the benefits of communicating them.

Notice how you feel in this scenario: Are you anxious about appearing unprepared? Are you worried about what others might think? Emphasizing these feelings helps you to recognize and acknowledge your emotions, which is a crucial step in learning to advocate for yourself.

Now, imagine a different course of action. Instead of staying silent, visualize yourself taking a deep breath and raising your hand or walking over to the teacher (or adult), initiating the conversation to ask for help. You're making eye contact, speaking clearly, and using "I" statements to express your needs, such as, "I'm having trouble understanding this. Can you explain it again, maybe in a different way?" or, "I feel I would benefit from having an extra day to focus on this project to ensure it meets our high standards."

Finally, imagine yourself reflecting on the experience of speaking up. Regardless of the outcome, visualize yourself recognizing the strength it took to advocate for your needs.

Rehearsal and application scenario:

Joyleen has a hard time following along and understanding what is being taught in class. This results in her failing tests repeatedly, and the teacher thinks she just doesn't care.

Wrong way to respond? Right way to respond?

Student-created scenario:

Wrong way to respond? Right way to respond?

continued →

Targeted life skill: GOAL SETTING

Motivation Academy

Definition: The ability to set time-targeted objectives and determine an action plan and the steps necessary to achieve them

Replacement behaviors:

Visualize goal and action plan—Imagine what you are trying to accomplish and by when (today, this week, this month, this year, and so on). For example, your goal might be related to improving a grade by the end of the quarter, decreasing the number of tardies you have this week, passing a class this semester, graduating from high school this year, and so on.

Now, think about your action plan. What will be your first steps toward the goal? For example, if your goal is to improve a grade by this quarter, a first step could be to look up your current grade along with the missing assignments, a next step would be to set up a meeting with the teacher to help get back on track, then an additional step would be to set up an hour block daily and work on catching up in class.

Goal signposts—A signpost is a verbal or physical marker that helps indicate clues and progress toward completing a goal. A person driving a car out of town may see physical and mental signposts toward their goal destination. Imagine and set signposts toward your goal. For example, instead of you bringing your F to an A overnight, you may set some signposts, such as, "In two weeks, if I turn in all of my assignments, I can bring up my grade to a C with the support of the teacher."

Rehearsal and application scenario:

Valentina does not know how to set goals for herself based on the class expectations. She also tends to cut corners, which results in incomplete work or having to redo work.

Wrong way to respond? Right way to respond?

Student-created scenario:

Wrong way to respond? Right way to respond?

Targeted life skill: **SELF-CONCEPT**

Motivation Academy

Definition: The ability to understand perceptions and beliefs about oneself (positive or negative)

Replacement behaviors:

Challenge negative self-thoughts—Negative thoughts sometimes pop up and make us feel bad about ourselves. When you have negative self-thoughts, challenge your negative thoughts by talking nicely about yourself, telling yourself the thoughts are not true, and that you can do it.

Self-portrait (strengths and weaknesses)—A self-portrait is typically a picture a person paints or draws or a description they write based on how they see themselves. Imagine a self-portrait of yourself, and be honest about what you see. How would you describe yourself, specifically your strengths and weaknesses? Acknowledge and accept your strengths and weaknesses. Everyone has strengths and weaknesses. Focus on your strengths to continue to grow.

Rehearsal and application scenario:

Mark focuses on what he lacks rather than what he has, which makes him feel bad about himself.

Wrong way to respond? Right way to respond?

Student-created scenario:

Wrong way to respond? Right way to respond?

Emotional Regulation Academy
Behavior Rehearsal Cards

Emotional Regulation Academy is designed for students who are struggling with emotions impacting learning (that is, shutdowns, eloping, and emotional outbursts). See the eight targeted life skills that align with the Emotional Regulation Academy along with the corresponding behavior rehearsal cards (see table 4.8 and figure 4.8).

TABLE 4.8: Emotional Regulation Academy At-A-Glance

Behavior Academy	Eight Targeted Life Skills	Replacement Behaviors
Emotional Regulation Academy	**Emotional expression:** The ability to express your feelings through verbal and nonverbal communication, actions, and behaviors and manage your feelings in an appropriate way	Mental journal Get it out of your system
	Self-awareness: The ability to recognize and understand your own thoughts, feelings, perspectives, strengths, weaknesses, and motivations and how you react to a variety of situations	Bear in the campground Pinpointing the root cause
	Self-regulation: The ability to be aware of your thoughts and emotions and how to manage them in a productive manner during challenging situations	Internal temperature (temp check) Balloon visual (pop it or let it go)
	Mindfulness: The ability to be present in the moment and have an awareness of one's thoughts, feelings, and surrounding environment	Practice acceptance of uncomfortable feelings Grounding safe space
	Help seeking: The ability to recognize and actively seek support and guidance from trusted individuals when faced with difficulties or challenges	Identify your stuck point (gum) Internal help signal
	Coping: The ability to manage stressful situations and challenges in an effective way	Assuring self-talk Challenge the negative thought trap with evidence
	Emotional literacy: The ability to recognize, identify, and respond appropriately to a range of one's own emotions and the emotions of others	Emotional mirror Fluent in naming your emotions
	Resilience: The ability to move forward or bounce back after facing a difficult situation, event, or challenge	Practice gratitude minute Glimmers finder

Targeted life skill: **EMOTIONAL EXPRESSION**

Emotional Regulation Academy

Definition: The ability to express your feelings through verbal and nonverbal communication, actions, and behaviors and manage your feelings in an appropriate way

Replacement behaviors:

Mental journal—Journaling helps people gain control over their thoughts, emotions, and feelings by writing them down in the moment. Imagine having a "mental journal" you can go to anytime you feel a need to express your emotions—a clean slate where you can imagine writing, drawing, scribbling, and so on. A physical journal works as well, but in the event you do not have one handy, the same concept can take place through your mental imagery.

Get it out of your system—Begin by visualizing a soda can sitting still. This represents your neutral state, where your emotions are in balance, and there's no pressure building inside of you. Now, imagine someone forcefully shaking the soda can. Each shake represents a stressor or emotional stimulus, like an upsetting incident, a hurtful comment, or an unmet expectation.

The more the can is shaken, the more pressure builds up inside, much like our emotions build up inside us when we're stressed, angry, or upset and keeping it all in. If you open a soda can soon after all the shaking, it will explode and make a mess. This can symbolize our impulsive reactions. Without any pause or reflection, or getting our feelings out in a positive way, it can lead to an explosion.

Imagine a soda can when you are trying to hold in emotions and push yourself to get it out of your system in a healthy way that works for you (that is, inside scream, say it out loud to someone, and so on).

Rehearsal and application scenario:

Pat is feeling angry at a scenario with a friend from lunch but is having a hard time expressing himself. He is obsessing over what happened and cannot concentrate on anything else.

Wrong way to respond? Right way to respond?

Student-created scenario:

Wrong way to respond? Right way to respond?

FIGURE 4.8: Emotional Regulation Academy behavior rehearsal cards.

continued →

Targeted life skill: SELF-AWARENESS

Emotional Regulation Academy

Definition: The ability to recognize and understand your own thoughts, feelings, perspectives, strengths, weaknesses, and motivations and how you react to a variety of situations

Replacement behaviors:

Bear in the campground—Imagine a real bear showing up in the campground you are at. What would you feel? It is a normal reaction to be afraid of a real-life bear (real threat) in your campground. However, sometimes we create bears in our campgrounds (threats, worries, fears) in our lives that aren't really there. A bear in a campground is one way of thinking about whether what you are worried, anxious, or upset about is a real threat or a "what if" scenario that is out of your control.

When you notice your feelings, identify if there is a real bear in the campground, or if you are putting bears in your life where they shouldn't be, by self-reflecting on the situation in your mind.

Pinpointing the root cause—Pinpoint means to locate exactly where something is coming from and, in this case, the root cause behind why you are feeling this way. Think of a recent situation where you experienced a strong emotional reaction. Visualize this scene as if you're watching a movie, trying to be a detached observer rather than a participant. In your visualization, pause the scene at the moment you felt a strong emotion. Identify this emotion (pinpoint)—anger, sadness, fear, and so on. Ask yourself, "What exactly am I feeling?" Imagine taking a pin and pinpointing it so you know what and where it is in the future.

Delve deeper into this emotion (root cause). Imagine a symbolic object in your safe space that represents this feeling. It could be a storm cloud for anger, a heavy rock for sadness, and so on. Ask the symbol questions: Why are you here? What are you protecting me from?

Listen for answers from your subconscious. Often, our emotional root causes are linked to past experiences. Imagine a pathway leading from the symbol to a door. Open this door to reveal a memory related to your current feelings. Observe this memory as a detached spectator, looking for insights. In your visualization, try to understand how this past experience influences your current reactions. Are you projecting past fears or hurts onto present situations?

With this new understanding, visualize yourself in a future situation like the emotional event. See yourself reacting in a more aware, controlled manner.

Rehearsal and application scenario:

Simon is feeling anxious but does not know why. This feeling is bothering him so much, and he does not know why or what is making him feel this way, but he does not like it. It makes him want to shut down and not do anything.

Wrong way to respond? Right way to respond?

Student-created scenario:

Wrong way to respond? Right way to respond?

Targeted life skill: **SELF-REGULATION**

Emotional Regulation Academy

Definition: The ability to be aware of your thoughts and emotions and how to manage them in a productive manner during challenging situations

Replacement behaviors:

Internal temperature (temp check)—Imagine a thermometer being used to take the temperature of an object or person. The temperature it is reading is how cold or hot something is. Imagine if you control your internal temperature and adjust it when you notice your body changing during a challenging situation. For example, when you feel yourself getting physically hot (that is, upset or angry), you will be able to use your strategies and turn the temperature down.

Balloon visual (pop it or let it go)—Imagine a balloon that represents a challenging situation or thought that is upsetting you. Imagine yourself popping the balloon (the thought of acting on it right away when you notice it). You can also decide to let the balloon fly away (let the thought or feeling go).

Rehearsal and application scenario:

Delia is having a rough day, and it keeps getting worse. She is holding in everything that is bothering her and is having a difficult time self-regulating. When her teacher gives her a directive later in the day to take out her materials and get to work, she screams, "Leave me alone!" and walks out of the classroom.

Wrong way to respond? Right way to respond?

Student-created scenario:

Wrong way to respond? Right way to respond?

continued →

Targeted life skill: **MINDFULNESS**

Emotional Regulation Academy

Definition: The ability to be present in the moment and have an awareness of one's thoughts, feelings, and surrounding environment

Replacement behaviors:

Practice acceptance of uncomfortable feelings— Emotions can make us feel good, and they can also make us feel bad or uncomfortable at times. Sometimes, when emotions feel uncomfortable, we struggle to accept them. When you feel this way, imagine sitting in your emotions instead of running away from them or letting your emotions run through you like a stream of water. The sooner you accept them, the sooner you can help your body respond. Tell yourself it is OK to feel what you are feeling and give yourself permission to sit and accept the uncomfortable feelings until they run through your system.

Grounding safe space—When you find yourself feeling anxiety, stress, or emotionally dysregulated, utilize your five senses (see, hear, smell, feel, and taste) to help you stay present and grounded. Identify the following.

5 Things You Can See: Look around and acknowledge five things that you can see. Pick something you don't usually notice, like a shadow or a small crack in the concrete.

4 Things You Can Feel: Pay attention to the things currently touching you and list four things you can feel. This could be the texture of your clothing, the feeling of the breeze on your skin, or the surface of the chair you are sitting in.

3 Things You Can Hear: Listen for and identify three sounds. It could be the sound of cars outside, the hum of the air conditioner, or the distant chirping of birds.

2 Things You Can Smell: Bring to mind two things that you can smell. If you can't immediately smell anything, walk nearby to sniff something, like a flower or an unlit candle.

1 Thing You Can Taste: Focus on one thing that you can taste right now, at this moment. You can take a sip of a drink, chew gum, eat something, notice the current taste in your mouth, or even open your mouth to search the air for a taste.

By engaging all of your senses, you are redirecting your focus away from distress, anxiety, or intrusive thoughts and providing a calming effect on your nervous system.

Rehearsal and application scenario:

Tera is feeling emotional about a scenario that took place with her best friend. Her best friend unfriended her from their social media application and is ignoring her at school. Tera is struggling to understand why her best friend is treating her this way and struggling to stop crying every time she thinks about it, which is often.

Wrong way to respond? Right way to respond?

Student-created scenario:

Wrong way to respond? Right way to respond?

Targeted life skill: **HELP SEEKING**

Emotional Regulation Academy

Definition: The ability to recognize and actively seek support and guidance from trusted individuals when faced with difficulties or challenges

Replacement behaviors:

Identify your stuck point (gum)—Imagine a piece of gum stuck to your shoe. Once you notice the gum, you work on ways to get it off your shoe. Now, think about when you feel stuck for a period of time (similar to gum stuck to your shoe). It is important to recognize it and ask for help to get out of your stuck spot.

Internal help signal—Imagine a low-battery signal on a device. This low-battery signal gives you a reminder to charge the device. Imagine an "internal help signal" for yourself (it can be similar to the low-battery signal we are all familiar with). When you see your signal alert you, it signals you to ask for help. For example, you may ask a teacher for a break or extra time, and so on.

Rehearsal and application scenario:

Joan feels herself becoming overwhelmed in class but does not know how to ask for help; to avoid accountability, she raises her hand to go to the bathroom and does not return until the bell rings.

Wrong way to respond? Right way to respond?

Student-created scenario:

Wrong way to respond? Right way to respond?

continued →

Targeted life skill: COPING

Emotional Regulation Academy

Definition: The ability to manage stressful situations and challenges in an effective way

Replacement behaviors:

Assuring self-talk: Assuring self-talk helps us feel more assured that we can get through a challenging situation or emotions we are experiencing. Thoughts influence feelings and behavior. Our beliefs about ourselves often become self-fulfilling prophecies. Imagine talking to yourself during these times and continuously saying statements such as "I am going to be OK," "Everything is going to be OK," and "It will get better over time."

Challenge the negative thought trap with evidence—Imagine a negative thought being like a trap. A trap catches you and is hard to get out of. Challenge the negative thought trap with evidence. Using evidence will help you stop the trap or release you from the trap. For example, if your negative thought is telling you, "Your emotions are in control of you, and there is no way you can feel better or overcome them," you can challenge the negative thought trap with, "I can learn new skills to help me cope during difficult times, like the other day when I became extremely upset and used my skills during an interaction that took place in one of my classes."

It may take multiple attempts to challenge the negative thought trap, but do not give up.

Rehearsal and application scenario:

Darren is extremely upset about a grade he received on an important project in class. He begins feeling his heart rate increase and feels completely hopeless and worried about telling his parents.

Wrong way to respond? Right way to respond?

Student-created scenario:

Wrong way to respond? Right way to respond?

Targeted life skill: **EMOTIONAL LITERACY**

Emotional Regulation Academy

Definition: The ability to recognize, identify, and respond appropriately to a range of one's own emotions and the emotions of others

Replacement behaviors:

Emotional mirror—Imagine having a mirror that will help you identify (see) a range and patterns of your emotions. Pull out your emotional mirror to help you identify your emotions and assure yourself they are OK to have.

Fluent in naming your emotions—When someone is fluent at something, it typically means they are really good at it. Imagine being fluent in naming your own emotions. For example, when you are feeling emotional about something, try to name the emotion that is making you feel that way as your first step. The more you practice, the more fluent you will become at not only naming your emotions, but being able to assure yourself you are going to get through it.

Rehearsal and application scenario:

Kayden gets into a disagreement with his coach. He is feeling tons of emotions at the same time, specifically angry and wanting to quit.

Wrong way to respond? Right way to respond?

Student-created scenario:

Wrong way to respond? Right way to respond?

continued →

Targeted life skill: **RESILIENCE**

Emotional Regulation Academy

Definition: The ability to move forward or bounce back after facing a difficult situation, event, or challenge

Replacement behaviors:

Practice gratitude minute—*Gratitude* is defined as being thankful for the good things in your life, such as small or big moments, things you have, and the people in your life. During challenging situations, it is difficult to focus on what we are grateful for (the good things we have) and easier to focus on what we do not have. When you are feeling discouraged, picture in your head at least three to five good small or big moments, things you have or people in your life you are grateful for. Do this for at least one minute daily to help you find the strength to bounce back. This will also help interrupt the focus on what you do not have and shift the focus to what you do have.

It is recommended that you practice gratitude for one minute daily to help in general, even when not experiencing challenging situations.

Glimmers finder—Glimmers are the opposite of triggers and help build resilience. Glimmers are small happy moments and memories that help make your nervous system feel safe and hopeful when you find yourself in a difficult situation. Finding glimmers when you are feeling down or in general is a helpful healing practice. Everyone has different glimmers; try to imagine some you can pull from. Some examples of glimmers include having a good talk with a close friend or teacher, being outside feeling the sun and breathing fresh air, having time to think, and so on. Imagine your glimmers and find them when you need them.

Rehearsal and application scenario:

Tyron is feeling like he is failing with his friends, with his family, and at school. His feelings are compounding, and he feels like there is no way this will ever get better for him. He feels down and numb at school and at home.

Wrong way to respond? Right way to respond?

Student-created scenario:

Wrong way to respond? Right way to respond?

*Visit **go.SolutionTree.com/behavior/BA** for a free reproducible version of this figure.*

In chapter 5, we provide the phases to help you build your own behavior academy.

Chapter 5

Build Your Own Behavior Academy

Internalize it so you can lead it.

—Jessica and John Hannigan

The highest level of mastery with behavior academy implementation comes when you have internalized the thinking behind behavior academies and apply it to build your own behavior academy when necessary. At this level, you may take the thinking behind the specific replacement behaviors we have provided and expand them beyond the sixteen in each academy to provide additional offerings on your campus. You'll be able to adapt the rehearsals and application scenarios based on the targeted age of the students you serve and based on the specific interests of your students to make the scenarios even more relevant. You may even wish to develop a separate academy beyond the eight provided. Once you internalize the thinking behind visualization and mental imagery exercises used to teach replacement behaviors, you've reached a point of endless possibilities for your students.

We want to reiterate a couple of key points for intentional redundancy before continuing. First, in chapter 3 (page 25), we provided the behavior academy structure in its most formalized fashion: the initial session, ongoing sessions, and exit session. In chapter 4 (page 57), we then introduced you to a series of ready-made behavior academy rehearsal cards for each of the eight behavior academies to help teach students targeted life skills in an effective, practical way. Through these two chapters alone, you have a systematic process and an abundance of tools within each rehearsal card. However, what if you want to create your own behavior academy, and specifically, new targeted behavior academy rehearsal cards for the ongoing sessions component of the academy? What if you want to address additional focus areas beyond the eight behavior academies we provided, such as anger management, social aggression, or making friends? Where would you begin?

As you build your own behavior academy, the behavior academy structure we have provided remains consistent—initial session, ongoing sessions, and exit session. However, the content of the behavior academy ongoing sessions (what to teach) needs to match the behavior focus area of the academy you wish to develop. In this chapter, we provide the frame to build your own behavior academy rehearsal cards, complete with a blank behavior rehearsal card template to insert your final product.

There are four phases for building a new behavior academy, as illustrated in figure 5.1, which captures the thinking at-a-glance as you begin to create new behavior academy rehearsal cards with targetedness in mind.

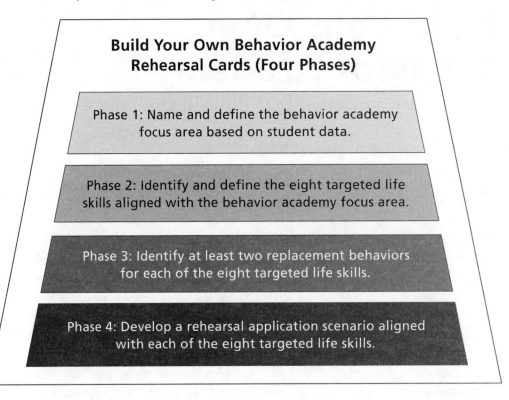

Build Your Own Behavior Academy Rehearsal Cards (Four Phases)

Phase 1: Name and define the behavior academy focus area based on student data.

Phase 2: Identify and define the eight targeted life skills aligned with the behavior academy focus area.

Phase 3: Identify at least two replacement behaviors for each of the eight targeted life skills.

Phase 4: Develop a rehearsal application scenario aligned with each of the eight targeted life skills.

FIGURE 5.1: Build your own behavior academy rehearsal cards (four phases) graphic.

In figure 5.2, we provide a guide to support building your own behavior academy rehearsal cards that covers all four phases and will help keep you organized as we explain how to build out each phase. (See page 177 for a reproducible version of this figure.) Complete the corresponding section of this build-your-own behavior academy (four phases) guide *as you read each phase.* If you complete this guide now, there will be sections that won't make sense. We will explain each phase as you read on. However, by the end of phase four, you will be at a place where you can transfer the collective information to your very own behavior rehearsal card template and will be ready to implement your newly created behavior academy.

Phase	Provide Evidence of This Phase
Phase 1: Name and define the behavior academy focus area based on student data.	Name of the behavior academy: Definition of the behavior academy: What data was utilized to decide this is a necessary behavior academy?
Phase 2: Identify and define the eight targeted life skills aligned with the behavior academy focus area.	List the eight targeted life skills aligned with the behavior academy: _____ _____ _____ _____ _____ _____ _____ _____ How did you identify the eight targeted life skills using the following three-pronged approach? Consider these questions as you determine your answer. 1. Did you collaborate with the teachers and other educators to capture the eight targeted life skills you want students to improve on? 2. Did you research the various life skills necessary for appropriately managing one's anger? 3. Did you leverage the collective expertise and experience in your building or district (staff who have a background or training in managing the behavior)?

FIGURE 5.2: Build your own behavior academy rehearsal cards (four phases) guide.   continued →

Phase 3:
Identify at least
two replacement
behaviors for each
of the eight targeted
life skills.

List the eight targeted life skills and two replacement behaviors for each life skill.

Life Skill: _____

Replacement Behavior 1: _____

Replacement Behavior 2: _____

Life Skill: _____

Replacement Behavior 1: _____

Replacement Behavior 2: _____

Life Skill: _____

Replacement Behavior 1: _____

Replacement Behavior 2: _____

Life Skill: _____

Replacement Behavior 1: _____

Replacement Behavior 2: _____

Life Skill: _____

Replacement Behavior 1: _____

Replacement Behavior 2: _____

Life Skill: _____

Replacement Behavior 1: _____

Replacement Behavior 2: _____

Life Skill: _____

Replacement Behavior 1: _____

Replacement Behavior 2: _____

Life Skill: _____

Replacement Behavior 1: _____

Replacement Behavior 2: _____

How did you decide on the replacement behaviors for each of the eight targeted life skills?

What will you be utilizing to teach the replacement behaviors (imagery and visualization exercises, existing lessons from behavior curriculum or resources your school has, creating your own, and so on)?

Phase 4: Develop a rehearsal application scenario aligned with each of the eight targeted life skills.	List the eight targeted life skills. Insert a short scenario for application practice next to each: Life Skill: _____ Scenario: _____ Life Skill: _____ Scenario: _____ Life Skill: _____ Scenario: _____ Life Skill: _____ Scenario: _____ Life Skill: _____ Scenario: _____ Life Skill: _____ Scenario: _____ Life Skill: _____ Scenario: _____ Life Skill: _____ Scenario: _____ How did you create the scenarios?

This chapter walks you through the four phases of building your own behavior rehearsal cards we covered in the previous chapter and how they are applied, using anger management as an example. At the end of each phase, we will ask you to reflect using this build-your-own behavior academy rehearsal cards (four phases) guide. You can reflect using this chapter's example of anger management in each phase, or you can insert your own targeted behavior focus area and begin the building process.

Phase 1: Name and Define the Behavior Academy Focus Area Based on Student Data

In phase 1, it is important to name and define the behavior academy focus area based on student data. This phase is all about developing clarity based on need because you are using student data (the area of need) as the starting point to develop a new set of behavior rehearsal cards. For example, if behavior data show students are expressing anger through verbal assaults, destruction of property, or the most overt form of anger expression, physical aggression, we would create and name the *Anger Management Academy*. We would next need to define the purpose: *The Anger Management Academy is designed to help students identify their emotions and triggers as well as how they express and manage that anger appropriately.*

At this point, reflect on phase 1 and capture your thinking using the build-your-own behavior academy rehearsal cards (four phases) guide in figure 5.2 (page 133).

Phase 2: Identify and Define the Eight Targeted Life Skills Aligned With the Behavior Academy Focus Area

In this second phase, you need to identify and define eight targeted life skills necessary for students to practice and demonstrate so they can manage anger appropriately. For example, some targeted life skills for anger management can include but are not limited to identifying anger triggers, self-regulation, self-awareness, and so on. Remember, we recommend at least eight targeted life skills because we recommend at least one new targeted life skill a week for six to eight weeks to help students rehearse and apply these skills over time.

We use the following three-pronged approach to identify eight targeted life skills for each behavior academy,

1. Collaborate with the teachers and other educators to capture the eight targeted life skills you want students to improve on. For example, we gather stakeholder input on what behaviors they want to see instead.

2. Research the various life skills necessary for appropriately managing one's anger. For example, we study research articles regarding best practices for managing anger.

3. Leverage the collective expertise and experience in your building or district (staff who have a background or training in behavior). For example, we would talk to the people who went to school for exactly this to gather resources and suggestions from them.

By addressing this process from three different angles, you are being comprehensive and collaborative, which leads to ownership from the stakeholders involved in supporting the delivery of the behavior academy.

Once you identify the eight targeted life skills, you must collaboratively define each one. For example, *identifying anger triggers* is the ability to recognize your body's reactions and understand the situations and experiences that lead to these negative reactions and behaviors. The importance of having clarity and consensus around these definitions is critical because the two replacement behaviors (detailed in the next section) will teach the student to do exactly what has been defined. Therefore, if it is unclear or there isn't agreement on the definition for each targeted life skill, the replacement behaviors students must learn to demonstrate will be met with inconsistency—everyone will have varying ideas of a student's mastery of those skills and no clarity or consensus on the target.

At this point, reflect on phase 2 and capture your thinking using the build-your-own behavior academy rehearsal cards (four phases) guide in figure 5.2 (page 133).

Phase 3: Identify at Least Two Replacement Behaviors for Each of the Eight Targeted Life Skills

Phase 3 entails identifying the replacement behaviors to help students demonstrate the targeted skill. Replacement behaviors are easy to select (not to mention fun) and help students practice and demonstrate the targeted life skills. We need to provide replacement behaviors for the students to pull from as we increase the tools in their inner toolkits. For example, if *identifying anger triggers* is a targeted life skill for an anger management behavior academy, two replacement behaviors that could help students identify anger triggers can include but are not limited to: (1) name what your mind and body are telling you when you feel yourself becoming angry and (2) pinpoint what is upsetting you.

There are many ways you can identify replacement behaviors that are practical for students to pull from at any time. For example, you can identify the replacement behaviors from your own experiences, preexisting district-adopted behavior curriculum, research, ChatGPT or other generative AI tools, stakeholder input, and utilizing the behavior experts in your school or district, to name a few.

When we are selecting replacement behaviors for behavior academy rehearsal cards, as mentioned prior in this book, we like to lean toward imagery or visualization-based replacement behaviors when possible. For example, for a student to improve on the targeted life skill of identifying emotional triggers, they need some replacement behaviors to help. One replacement behavior for identifying emotional triggers might be *name what your mind and body are telling you*. This replacement behavior requires a student to imagine or visualize through their senses what they are feeling, hearing, seeing, and so on in order to see and name what triggered their anger response. With this self-understanding, the student can be more preventative when noticing that same (or even a new) emotional trigger in the future.

At this point, reflect on phase 3 and capture your thinking using the build-your-own behavior academy rehearsal cards (four phases) guide in figure 5.2 (page 133).

Phase 4: Develop a Rehearsal Application Scenario Aligned With Each of the Eight Targeted Life Skills

In phase 4, it is important to develop application (rehearsal) opportunities. Start by developing a behavior rehearsal scenario, similar to those outlined in the chapter 4 (page 57) behavior rehearsal cards to help students practice the application of the replacement behaviors from each of the eight targeted life skills. Make sure the scenario is related to the targeted focus area; in this case, identifying anger triggers. Using the example of the Anger Management Academy and the specific targeted life skill of *identifying anger triggers,* a scenario could be as follows.

> *Sarah was having a difficult time with her mathematics assignment. With every problem seeming harder than the last, she was becoming more and more frustrated and angry. Her classmate kept on saying how easy it was, which made Sarah start to think that the classmate was implying she was stupid because it was more difficult for her. Feeling her face become hot and her heart rate increase, Sarah snapped at her classmate, "Get out of my face and stop talking to me!"*

This scenario or a similar one should help guide the conversation of what would be an appropriate (right way) and inappropriate (wrong way) response. And specifically, what replacement behaviors a student can apply to that scenario.

You can create scenarios based on your own experiences, using existing behavior curriculum, real-life experiences you've heard colleagues talk about, ChatGPT or other generative AI based on any prompts you ask it, stakeholder input, or leveraging the behavior experts at the school or district. If time permits, have the students identify an additional scenario they directly relate to, as well, to rehearse and practice their newly learned skills. You can also add their student-created scenarios to your academies for use in the future with other students.

At this point, reflect on phase 4 and capture your thinking using the build-your-own behavior academy rehearsal cards (four phases) guide in figure 5.2.

It is not easy to develop new behavior academy rehearsal cards from scratch; it takes intentionality and thought. However, once developed, you will have an additional behavior academy beyond the eight in this book to use when students demonstrate a need for that new focus area. Eventually, you will have a bank of behavior academies to utilize as needed. Simply follow the four phases we model in this chapter, then transfer that information into the behavior rehearsal card template in figure 5.3, using a single-page blank template for each life skill, and you will have ready-to-go behavior rehearsal cards for each ongoing session. (See page 180 for a reproducible version of this figure.)

Front of Behavior Rehearsal Card	Back of Behavior Rehearsal Card
Definition:	**Rehearsal and application scenario:**
Replacement behaviors:	Wrong way to respond? Right way to respond?
	Student-created scenario:
	Wrong way to respond? Right way to respond?

Targeted life skill: / Academy

FIGURE 5.3: Behavior rehearsal card template.

We are certain you will have some questions as you have processed all the information covered so far in this book. In chapter 6, we will provide our most frequently asked questions and responses.

Chapter 6

Behavior Academy Frequently Asked Questions and Additional Tools

Everything shared in this book is based on the needs we hear from educators across the United States. It's written by practitioners for practitioners. The information is not based on theory but on proven practices. While the preceding chapters provide all the actionable guidance you need to not only implement behavior academies effectively but also understand the thinking behind behavior academies, we think it's also vital that you have quick answers to frequently asked questions. In this chapter, we include some of the most frequently asked questions we receive and our responses, along with some additional tools that may be helpful. Read this in its entirety as a comprehensive overview of frequently asked questions related to behavior academies or use it as a quick-reference tool to find fast answers to questions you encounter when implementing this work.

Who can deliver behavior academies?

We designed behavior academies and specifically the behavior rehearsal cards aligned with each behavior academy as an easy, practical, and effective way for any educator to be empowered to provide additional targeted teaching and reteaching opportunities for students. We have seen teachers (in whole-class and small-group environments), administrators, behavior support providers, counselors, social workers, school psychologists, and even parents or guardians (with their own children at home) utilize our behavior academies to help teach and reteach targeted behaviors.

To coordinate the support system on your campus to deliver this work, take inventory of the human capital to reflect on the expertise in your building and the various roles and responsibilities they hold on your campus. Also, reflect on formal or informal delivery of behavior academies, as detailed in table 6.1. We recommend, in its most formalized delivery with all the components of the behavior academy structure, you lean toward the people who have the most specialty and experience with behavior.

TABLE 6.1: Differences Between Formal and Informal Delivery of Behavior Academies.

Formal	Informal
Sessions are delivered individually or in small groups and are based on data.	Instruction may be delivered to whole or small groups as necessary.
Frequency of lesson delivery is ongoing, at least once per week for six to eight weeks.	Frequency of lesson delivery is as needed.
Goals and progress monitoring are in place.	Goals and weekly progress monitoring structures may or may not be in place.

This is often where we see a rift in when targeted behavior support may begin. We'll hear, "Sounds great, but who is going to do that?" or various reasons why this work "cannot be done" on that campus. For example, we frequently see variations of the following scenarios.

▸ A high school counselor who says she can't see groups of students who need additional time and support because her job is to attend to schedule changes for students (office staff could do that with training)

▸ A counselor who is the 504 coordinator with seventy-five students on her caseload (an assistant principal can hold the responsibility of 504 coordinator)

▸ A school psychologist who says he only tests students for special education

▸ A school psychologist or behavior expert who is housed at the district office and not seen as part of a school's staff

The people in these positions are among the most well-trained staff on any campus, hired to support the most vulnerable students who are at risk of failure, so we ask, "*If not you, who? And if not now, when?*" If they are frustrated with the many additional tasks on their plates or have a "This is not part of my job description" sentiment, your campus needs to take an audit of how these specialists are spending their time each day. If support staff with critical training and expertise say they are unable to support this work on your campus, this will not work.

We are in no way saying that these specialists are not currently working tirelessly to support the students on your campus. We have, however, seen a variety of ways in which their skillset is misused, which creates a depletion of resources to support this work. Clearly defining roles and responsibilities is essential to delivering behavior academies well.

Table 6.2 captures various ways we see this multidisciplinary team of specialists (counselor, social worker, school psychologist, and other professionals) being misused on school campuses.

TABLE 6.2: Common Misuses of School Behavior Specialists

Role or Task	Factors to Avoid Misusing Behavior Specialists
Administrative tasks	Overuse or inconsistent administrative supervision assignments, proctoring exams, or primarily managing class schedules is an ineffective use of a behavior specialist's skills.
Discipline	Being brought in to handle disciplinary matters not only takes away time from supporting intervention groups, but students may begin to associate the behavior specialist's role with punishment.
Substitute teaching	Asking specialists to fill in as substitute teachers on a regular basis detracts from their primary role of providing services to students.
Exclusion from collaborative decision making	Specialists have specialized training in student behavior, emotions, and needs. The school may miss out on critical insights for prevention or early intervention by not including them in schoolwide decisions.
Not utilizing their comprehensive skillset (Counselors)	While school counselors are trained in academic advising and career counseling, they also have training in human development with knowledge about how to support students' social-emotional development, multicultural counseling, group counseling around grief, academic skills, and social skills, as well as crisis intervention.
Not utilizing their comprehensive skillset (Social workers)	While social workers serve as a link between schools and community resources, address chronic absenteeism, and provide support through home visits to gather additional information or address specific challenges, they are also trained in individual counseling, group counseling, crisis intervention, behavioral interventions, and prevention programs for issues such as bullying, substance abuse, and mental health.
Excessive testing (School psychologist)	Using the school psychologist solely for testing and assessment without utilizing this specialist's expertise in counseling, consultation, and behavioral intervention is a missed opportunity.
Large caseloads	If caseloads are too large, it diminishes the quality of the services behavior specialists provide for each student. A lack of Tier 1 prevention on a campus is the main contributing factor to high caseloads.
Inadequate placement	If behavior specialists are housed at the district office and not on a school campus, it can lead to a mismatch between the services provided and the school's actual needs.
Crisis-only approach	If behavior specialists are only utilized in times of crisis or with the most extreme needs, it prevents proactive, preventive work with students who might be at risk.

To avoid outcomes like those listed in table 6.2, take a human resource inventory of this team of specialists on your campus. List their roles and responsibilities and how much time is allocated to some of these misuses we highlighted. If their reason for not being available to support the work of behavior academies is due to any of the misuses (or any similar misuses you observe), you will need to assess a fair division of labor within the human capital you have available on your campus. These are your most highly skilled personnel to support behavior. Students will undoubtedly elevate to a higher risk if we wait for them to continue to struggle and will most certainly become a priority for this team once they reach the most intensive level of support needed.

So, if not you, who? And if not now, when?

When do we schedule behavior academies?

When providing additional time and targeted support for behavior is a priority, whoever is providing the support will allocate the time to do so. Any supports cannot be optional or left to chance; they need to be scheduled and built into the bell schedule within the school day for students and contractual duty day for staff. We outline various ways schools can implement behavior academies (formally and informally) in this section.

For example, classroom teachers can use behavior rehearsal cards with their entire class or a small group of students within their class, grade level, or department demonstrating a need to learn and rehearse newly learned life skills. Most often, we see this happen during a designated behavior block required schoolwide for all teachers. Some schools have a designated thirty-minute block per week for social and emotional learning lessons and/or advisory, homeroom, and college career readiness. We have also seen teachers implement designated intervention blocks such as WIN time and so on.

However, a schoolwide systematic response based on data to identify students in need of additional support requires additional layers of behavioral expertise to help. Specifically, the multidisciplinary group of educators that were highlighted in the previous section should be planning for this in their schedules, and a school- or district-wide culture needs to be created and maintained to ensure their schedule is protected to do so.

Next, we provide a few schoolwide behavior academy schedule samples (elementary, middle school, and high school) to help conceptualize how this might work for your school. The first is an elementary example (see figure 6.1). To give you some context, every morning (the first thirty minutes) starts with schoolwide announcements, classroom meetings, and schoolwide behavior lessons or exercises for the purpose of prevention. This school also has a daily built-in academic intervention block on Mondays, Tuesdays, Thursdays, and Fridays, but it has intentionally added a behavior intervention block on Wednesdays. In addition, this school has a counselor on-site three days a week (Monday, Wednesday, and Friday, seven hours a day) who helps with behavior academy delivery on those days. The vice principal (five days a week) and the MTSS lead teacher (five days a week) also help with behavior academy delivery throughout the week; they are all members of the smaller behavior intervention team on the campus as well. Note the behavior academies take twenty-five minutes or less, but the school added five minutes to account for the students coming to and leaving the behavior academy depending on where it is taking place.

Monday	Tuesday	Wednesday	Thursday	Friday
8:00–8:30 a.m. Social Skills Academy (Counselor)		8:00–8:30 a.m. Emotional Regulation Academy (Counselor)		8:00–8:30 a.m. Emotional Regulation Academy (Counselor)
8:30–9:00 a.m. Upstander Academy Group (Counselor)	8:30–9:00 a.m. Hands-Off Academy (Vice Principal)	8:30–9:00 a.m. Upstander Academy Group (Counselor)	8:30–9:00 a.m. Hands-Off Academy (Vice Principal)	8:30–9:00 a.m. Social Skills Academy (Counselor)
Younger Lunch—Social Skills Academy (Counselor)		Older Lunch—Social Skills Academy (Counselor)		
1:00–1:30 p.m. Intervention (Academic) Block	1:00–1:30 p.m. Intervention (Academic) Block	1:00–1:30 p.m. Intervention (Behavior) Block Upstander Academy (Counselor) 1:00–1:30 p.m. Intervention (Behavior) Block Organizational Academy (MTSS Lead Teacher) 1:00–1:30 p.m. Intervention (Behavior) Block Organizational Academy (Teachers based on grade level needs can deliver)	1:00–1:30 p.m. Intervention (Academic) Block	1:00–1:30 p.m. Intervention (Academic) Block

FIGURE 6.1: Sample elementary school behavior academy delivery schedule.

As you can see from figure 6.1, the schedule is inclusive of the counselor, vice principal, and MTSS lead (twelve slots for behavior academy delivery). If teachers work with their grade-level teams to identify academic behaviors impacting student outcomes, they can also implement them during this designated behavior intervention block, thus creating additional slots for students needing added time and support. If teachers are utilized in this schedule, our suggestion is they take the lead on the academic-based behavior interventions, such as organizational skills, time management, goal setting, and work completion, to name a few, and not the social behaviors, such as anger management, social skills, and upstander (again, to name a few).

Figure 6.2 is an example of a middle school schedule. To provide context, this school has daily set advisory periods for seventh grade (before lunch) and eighth grade (after lunch). This allows the behavior intervention team on this site to provide support, and administrators who need to help with lunch supervision can do so. At this school, behavior academies are delivered specifically on Thursdays and Fridays during advisory periods. In this case, the counselor, administration team (the principal and two vice principals), and school psychologist help deliver behavior academies consistently on those days.

Monday	Tuesday	Wednesday	Thursday	Friday
11:30 a.m.–12:00 p.m. (seventh-grade advisory before lunch)—Schoolwide Advisory	11:30 a.m.–12:00 p.m. (seventh-grade advisory before lunch)—Schoolwide Advisory	11:30 a.m.–12:00 p.m. (seventh-grade advisory before lunch)—Schoolwide Advisory	11:30 a.m.–12:00 p.m. (seventh-grade advisory before lunch)—Behavior Academies (led by counselor, administrator team, school psychologist, and teachers)	11:30 a.m.–12:00 p.m. (seventh-grade advisory before lunch)—Behavior Academies (led by counselor, administrator team, school psychologist, and teachers)
12:50–1:20 p.m. (eighth-grade advisory after lunch)—Schoolwide Advisory	12:50–1:20 p.m. (eighth-grade advisory after lunch)—Schoolwide Advisory	12:50–1:20 p.m. (eighth-grade advisory after lunch)—Schoolwide Advisory	12:50–1:20 p.m. (eighth-grade advisory after lunch)—Behavior Academies (led by counselor, administrator team, school psychologist, and teachers)	12:50–1:20 p.m. (eighth-grade advisory after lunch)—Behavior Academies (led by counselor, administrator team, school psychologist, and teachers)

FIGURE 6.2: Sample middle school behavior academy delivery schedule.

The counselor takes the lead on the Social Skills Academy and Motivation Academy, the school psychologist takes the lead on the Emotional Regulation Academy, and the principal and the vice principals take the lead on the Hands-Off Academy and Upstander Academy. This schedule allows for at least four behavior academy delivery opportunities every Thursday and Friday from each of the behavior intervention team members, with a small group or individual students who need targeted additional support while teachers continue to provide prevention review or small-group reteaching of academic behaviors on Thursdays and Fridays during advisory. Like the elementary school in the previous example, this school has designated thirty minutes to allow for the coming and going from the behavior academy.

Figure 6.3 is an example of a high school schedule. The five counselors, the school psychologist, and the teacher mentor lead (also on their behavior intervention team) use the rotating schedule model provided to deliver behavior academies weekly. Staff rotate the periods students are pulled from for the twenty-five-minute academy sessions. For example, in week one, students are pulled during the last one-third of class. This ensures that all students have access to core instruction during the first two-thirds of that class period. For a seventy-five-minute period, students have fifty minutes of core instruction and the last twenty-five minutes for the behavior academy. A schedule will need to be drafted, and all staff (including campus monitors) will need to know which students are leaving and where they are going. This process ensures students are not pulled from the same period every week. The following week, period two is impacted with this schedule; the week after that, period three, and so on.

Behavior Academy Sessions	Period 1	Period 2	Period 3	Period 4	Period 5	Period 6	Period 7	Period 8
Week one	X							
Week two		X						
Week three			X					
Week four				X				
Week five					X			
Week six						X		
Week seven							X	
Week eight								X

FIGURE 6.3: Sample high school (rotating) behavior academy delivery schedule.

Note that if students are only pulled in period one, this penalizes all first-period staff by limiting them to only fifty minutes of instruction each week. We have also seen erroneous methods of pulling students from physical education, band, and electives. This does two negative things: (1) it silently communicates to those teachers that their content is not as important as others, and (2) you may be taking away one of the few classes that students love and look forward to each day. This process of rotating periods is one of the most equitable ways we have seen this done at the secondary level.

As illustrated in figure 6.4 (page 148), this same high school updated its overall bell schedule to include an advisory block (on Wednesdays) for thirty minutes designed for

Tuesday and Thursday Bell Schedule (intervention block and advisory)
Period 1
Period 2
Break
Intervention Block (Tuesday and Thursday) and Advisory (Wednesday)
Period 3
Period 4
Lunch
Period 5
Period 6
Period 7

FIGURE 6.4: Sample high school (intervention block and advisory) behavior academy delivery schedule.

schoolwide prevention supports on academic and social behaviors, and an intervention block two days a week for thirty minutes each day (Tuesdays and Thursdays) designed for additional targeted interventions provided by all members of the school staff. This provides an opportunity for the delivery of additional behavior academies in these designated slots by teachers and support staff.

Can we add new students to a behavior academy already in progress?

Yes. Let's say a new student needs a behavior academy, and you already have one running that an additional student would benefit from. You may decide to have some individual behavior academy sessions to catch them up, or you can have them join the academy in its current stage. The targeted life skills addressed in the behavior academies are not ordinal in any manner, so any student who joins later can remain longer to make up for the targeted skill focus sessions he or she missed.

Sometimes, new students mesh really well into an existing behavior academy group, and sometimes the behavior academy lead may need to start an individual or additional behavior academy group. Here is the only wrong way: you *cannot* wait six to eight weeks or until you end an existing behavior academy to provide students at risk of failure the additional time and support they need!

Do you deliver behavior academies to individual students or small groups?

You can deliver behavior academies to both individual students *and* in small groups. We have done both! Some students will respond to a small-group environment, and some will respond better to individual sessions. For example, you might opt for individual sessions for a student if you conduct a small-group session but notice that student is not feeling comfortable or is distracted by other students. Or you might use an individual delivery format for a student who takes over the small group or makes a mockery of the content because they have a captive audience in this small-group setting. These and other such behaviors are good indicators to adjust delivery format for the student to a more individualized fashion. This decision is up to the professional delivering the behavior academy. It can also be a conversation with the student. In most cases, students will respond to a small-group environment, but there are some cases where students may respond better to individual sessions; both are fine.

What is an ideal number of students for a small group?

If you are delivering a behavior academy in a small-group setting, we believe three to five students is an ideal group size. When groups become larger, it can make it difficult to provide the necessary attention each student needs while conducting the academy session within the twenty-five minutes allocated.

How often should behavior academy ongoing sessions be delivered and for how long?

We recommend each behavior academy ongoing session be delivered once or twice a week for twenty-five minutes per session. We want to keep it practical but efficient. We recommend allowing for at least six to eight weeks of implementation for students to be taught, rehearse, and generalize the newly learned skills. It takes time, as we previously mentioned, for students to demonstrate new productive habits and therefore requires consistent, ongoing support. As mentioned, this is why we give eight targeted life skills for each of our behavior academies—so educators can focus on one targeted life skill a week and then revisit them if students need more time and support. For example, if after eight weeks, eight targeted life skills are covered, yet students continue to demonstrate a need, consider bumping up the frequency of sessions, going back to previous life skills, and providing additional rehearsal and practice.

Do we need parent permission to provide behavior academies?

It depends. We start with this question: Is a permission slip sent home every time teachers provide additional reteaching of academic skills or standards for students who are not responding to first-best instruction? We are guessing the answer is *no*. We do recognize this topic is behavior, however, and since behavior academies may be delivered by other staff and not the classroom teacher (for example, the counselor, the social worker, or the school psychologist), it can elicit different reactions from families if the purpose and scope of the behavior academies are not explained correctly. We have gathered a few suggestions in the following list, but ultimately, your school or district's policy regarding parent permission will determine the direction you take.

- ▶ We recommend including language in the district and school parent and guardian handbooks about multitiered systems of academic and behavioral supports. This language should specifically emphasize that students will be provided both academics and behavior reteaching opportunities based on their needs, and one method for reteaching behavior is behavior academies. This is where the purpose and the design of the behavior academy can be explained to parents and guardians. This is also where the distinct difference between behavior academies (this work) and the more intensive one-to-one counseling or therapy can be clarified.

- ▶ Whether or not you use a permission slip to get started, we recommend informing the parent or guardian of the behavior academy their child is matched to based on data and the behaviors their child is demonstrating. We feel communication is always best practice. Parents and guardians can also be partners in this process and support their child with generalizing these newly learned skills at home.

- ▶ If someone other than the teacher is providing additional time and targeted behavior support and feels more comfortable with a permission slip being sent home for their own safeguarding, we have provided a sample behavior academy permission slip template in figure 6.5. (See page 181 for a reproducible version of this figure.) Tip: If the parent or guardian has not returned the permission slip in a timely manner, it is important for the lead delivering the behavior academy to make an effort to contact and help clarify any concerns for the parent or guardian and also ask for support from administration to help communicate with the parent or guardian.

Student's name: _____

Behavior academy name and description: _____

Behavior academy lead and contact information: _____

Behavior academy rationale:

_____

_____

_____

_____

_____

Starting date: _____   Ending date: _____ (TBD based on data)

I give permission for this behavior academy to be implemented.

Parent or guardian signature: _____ Date: _____

FIGURE 6.5: Sample behavior academy permission slip template.

What age levels are behavior academies for?

The structure for behavior academies is suitable for all age levels. No matter what grade level we work with, we try to accomplish the same thing; in other words, the thinking behind the behavior academy remains the same. We are providing more tools in their inner toolkits to help them with areas impacting their success. However, for younger students (preK through second grade), educators may include additional modalities (visuals, video clips, art, and so on) to help. They may simplify the definitions of the targeted life skills in developmentally appropriate language and modalities. Regardless of age, the structure remains the same: What are the targeted life skills you want students to demonstrate instead of the behaviors that made them candidates for the behavior academy in the first place?

How can behavior academies be utilized for prevention?

We know teachers who have used specific behavior rehearsal cards (one card each week) as a classwide prevention tool as we explained in some of the informal delivery methods of behavior academies previously in this book. We have seen some teachers do this during a social and emotional learning block, advisory period, WIN intervention time, and so on, as shown in the teacher lesson plan example we shared previously (figure 3.17, page 55).

How can you collect perception data for behavior academies, and how often?

Some behavior academies require perception data to help monitor. Perception data is based on stakeholder observations, experiences, interviews, and so on. One way to collect perception data is by using a short input survey given to teachers and other stakeholders at least once a week for the formalized implementation of behavior academies (which requires ongoing progress monitoring). For example, a counselor may deliver the behavior academy at least one time per week, and that same counselor asks for perception data input from a teacher observing to see if the student who is receiving the behavior academy is generalizing the new learned skills into the classroom setting.

You can also have a one-to-one conversation with the teacher and other stakeholders. In either case, the point is to collect information on students' progress and ability to generalize newly learned skills in their learning environment. For example, if a teacher was part of the referral process for a Social Skills Academy (noting a student struggling to make and sustain relationships with peers), then it would be important to hear from the teacher who referred the student in the first place to see if they are noticing the student applying the newly learned skills and making progress in the area of making and sustaining relationships with peers. See an example of a short, targeted intervention teacher and stakeholder input survey in figure 6.6. (See page 182 for a reproducible version of this figure.) This form of survey can be given to teachers in a paper or electronic format to complete. Tip: Keep it short and to the point.

Please complete this rating based on your perceptions and observations with the student this week. Remember to please rate based on the behavior focus (life skills) we have been focusing on in the behavior academy.

Student name: _____

Rate progress: _____

2 = Making progress

1 = Minimal progress

0 = No progress

Explain your rating in a few sentences:

FIGURE 6.6: Targeted intervention teacher and stakeholder input survey example.

How can we communicate what we are working on in the behavior academy with classroom teachers?

We often hear teachers say when students are pulled out of their classrooms that they do not know what the students are working on or how they can help. One way a behavior academy lead can provide a behavior academy ongoing session update is by filling out a quick at-a-glance form about a behavior academy session and giving it or sending it with the student to the teacher or stakeholder. See figure 6.7 for an example. (See page 183 for a blank reproducible version of this figure.) This is one way teachers can have the information they need to help students continue to generalize their newly learned skills and replacement behaviors in the classroom setting as well.

Student name: *Jared*	Behavior academy lead: *Mrs. T*	Date: *September 5, 2023*
Mark (X) targeted life skill session focus	**Hands-Off Academy targeted life skills**	**Ways a teacher or stakeholder can help:**
	Self-reflectiona	*Ask students to share what they learned (two-minute check-in).*
X	*Conflict resolution*	*Remind and reinforce these skills and replacement behaviors.*
	Impulse control	*Acknowledge and celebrate the wins you notice when students are applying their learned skills and replacement behaviors.*
	Identifying emotional triggers	
	Self-regulation	*Use the code word "activate" or a visual signal that serves as a reminder to the student to activate their newly learned skills and replacement behaviors when you notice the student needs a verbal or visual reminder to do so.*
	Accountability	
	Help seeking	
	Communication (verbal and nonverbal)	

FIGURE 6.7: Hands-Off Academy session at-a-glance example.

What is a behavior academy menu of interventions, and how can it help?

A *behavior academy menu* is a way to organize all the formalized behavior academies offered at your school. Remember, by *formalized* we mean all three components of the behavior academy structure are in place consistently. This form of a behavior academy menu is typically developed and delivered by the support staff members in addition to the teachers who have more specialty and expertise with behavior. This behavior academy menu also provides a nice overview of what is being offered schoolwide for teachers to have access to so there is clarity on what the students are receiving if they are enrolled in a behavior academy with a support provider on campus.

The behavior academy menu includes the name of the behavior academy, the description, the entrance criteria (ways students may be identified, matched, and access each behavior academy), and the exit criteria (criteria students need to meet with our support to exit the academy). The exit criteria options should correspond with the entrance criteria, meaning if a student was placed in the behavior academy because of some or all of the criteria listed in the entrance criteria, then the student should be exited based on improving in those criteria areas based on data. See figure 3.12 (page 46) for an example of a menu of exit criteria.

This is a good resource to help a school's behavior intervention team organize what each member offers. It will be easier to identify and match students based on data to an intervention if it is all in a centralized location and there is clarity of why each behavior academy was created in the first place. When deciding on entry and exit criteria, a school's behavior intervention team can decide how many menu items to provide and how many of them a student should meet. Figure 6.8, a behavior academy menu, is a good tool to develop and share with the entire staff so they see all the different behavior academies being offered. It also provides teachers with emotional safety, knowing that the school has a plan for any students demonstrating the behaviors that would make them candidates for the menu of academies provided.

Is there a tool that can provide additional support in helping educators match students to behavior academies?

Yes. We have a tool called the "Behavior Academy Matching Sheet (BAM-S)," which you can find as a reproducible in the appendix (page 184). This tool is a quick intervention matching form aligned with the eight behavior academies in this book. Educators can read each item and mark the agreement point value for each item accordingly for the student they have in mind. After the ratings are complete, the educator calculates the totals to see which behavior academies have the highest point totals. Note this is a reflection tool to help educators who may be stuck wondering which behavior academy may be a good match for a student. If the ratings indicate one or two options, you can retake the BAM-S, make a professional decision on where to begin, or both.

Through this chapter, we have provided you with the responses and additional tools to support the most frequently asked questions to help keep you on track for successful implementation.

Behavior Academy	Description	Entrance Criteria	Exit Criteria
Hands-Off Academy	Designed to help students struggling to keep their hands to themselves when they are angry or perceive a situation to be unfair	The student has challenges keeping their hands to themselves. The student has three or more discipline write-ups, referrals, or reports for putting hands on other students within a two-week period. A teacher, administrator, or support staff recommends the academy.	The student is consistently applying learned skills. The student has zero discipline write-ups, referrals, or reports for putting hands on other students consistently for a six- to eight-week period. A teacher, administrator, or support staff improved progress ratings.
Check-In Check-Out Academy	Designed for students struggling with repeated minor classroom misbehaviors	The student demonstrates repeated minor behavior challenges within the classroom (for example, disruptions, blurting out, difficulty staying on task, and so on). The student has three or more classroom-based discipline write-ups, referrals, or reports within a two-week period. A teacher, administrator, or support provider recommends the academy.	The student is consistently applying learned skills. The student has zero discipline write-ups, referrals, or reports for behavior challenges within the classroom consistently for a six- to eight-week period. The student meets CICO point card goals consistently for a six- to eight-week period. A teacher, administrator, or support provider improved progress ratings.
Civility Academy	Designed for students struggling to maintain civil discourse with other peers or adults who may have different points of view	The student has challenges with civil verbal interactions with peers or adults. The student has three or more discipline write-ups, referrals, or reports for negative verbal interactions with peers or adults within a two-week period. A teacher, administrator, or support staff recommends the academy.	The student is consistently applying learned skills. The student has zero discipline write-ups, referrals, or reports for negative verbal interactions with peers or adults consistently for a six- to eight-week period. A teacher, administrator, or support staff improved progress ratings.

FIGURE 6.8: Behavior academy menu.

continued →

Behavior Academy	Description	Entrance Criteria	Exit Criteria
Organizational Skills Academy	Designed for students struggling with organizational skills impacting readiness to learn and work completion	The student has challenges with keeping up with workload in class. The student has the ability and is trying to complete the work but easily gets overwhelmed and struggles to stay organized. The student is failing one or multiple courses or subjects within a two- or three-week grading period. A teacher, administrator, support provider, or parent recommends the academy. The student self-recommends the academy.	The student is consistently applying learned skills. The student is passing all courses or subjects consistently for a six- to eight-week period. A teacher, administrator, support staff, or parent improved progress ratings. The student improved their self-progress ratings.
Social Skills Academy	Designed for students struggling with appropriate peer or adult interactions	The student has challenges getting along with peers or adults inside and outside of the classroom. The student has three or more discipline write-ups, referrals, or reports related to this area within a two-week period. A teacher, administrator, support provider, or parent recommends the academy.	The student is consistently applying learned skills. The student has zero discipline write-ups, referrals, or reports in this area consistently for a six- to eight-week period. A teacher, administrator, support staff, or parent improved progress ratings.
Upstander Academy	Designed for students demonstrating or participating in bullying-type behaviors	The student is involved in (following along) or is leading bullying-type behaviors. The student has three or more discipline write-ups, referrals, or reports related to this area within a two-week period. The student's name has been reported repeatedly by other students or adults within a two-week period. A teacher, administrator, support provider, or parent recommends the academy. The student self-recommends the academy.	The student is consistently applying learned skills and removing themself from bullying-type behaviors and scenarios. The student has zero discipline write-ups, referrals, or reports for bullying-type behavior consistently for a six- to eight-week period. The student is no longer reported repeatedly by other students or adults for a six- to eight-week period. A teacher, administrator, support staff, or parent improved progress ratings. The student improved their self-progress ratings.

Behavior Academy	Description	Entrance Criteria	Exit Criteria
Motivation Academy	Designed for students who appear apathetic toward incomplete work, grades, and being in class on time	The student has challenges with attending and putting effort in academic coursework or subject areas. The student has three or more classroom-based discipline write-ups, referrals, or reports students for tardies or unexcused absences within a two-week period. The student is failing one or multiple courses or subjects within the grading period. A teacher, administrator, support staff, or parent recommends the academy. The student self-recommends the academy.	The student is consistently applying learned skills. The student has zero discipline write-ups, referrals, or reports for tardies and unexcused absences consistently for a six- to eight-week period. The student is passing all courses or subjects consistently for a six- to eight-week period. A teacher, administrator, support staff, or parent improved progress ratings. The student improved their self-progress ratings.
Emotional Regulation Academy	Designed for students who are struggling with emotions impacting learning (for example, shutdowns, eloping, emotional outbursts)	The student has challenges identifying emotions and using productive replacement behaviors. The student has three or more discipline write-ups, referrals, or reports for outbursts (that is, eloping, shutting down, screaming out, and so on) within a two-week period. A teacher, administrator, support staff, or parent recommends the academy. The student self-recommends the academy.	The student is consistently applying learned skills. The student has zero discipline write-ups, referrals, or reports for outbursts consistently for a six- to eight-week period. A teacher, administrator, support staff, or parent improved progress ratings. The student improved their self-progress ratings.

EPILOGUE

Do the best you can until you know better. Then, when you know better, do better.

—Maya Angelou

We want to extend our sincere gratitude and thank you for being relentless champions for students. We wrote this book to help educators simplify the complicated nature of targeted behavior interventions. Specifically, we wrote this book to address the challenges we captured in this book's introduction (page 1) with regard to impacting effective implementation of targeted interventions across the United States. We not only wanted to provide the thinking behind *why* implementation of behavior academies (targeted behavior interventions) is necessary in schools, proven to work, and practical, but also the *how* with easy-to-use tools in place to begin implementation right away no matter what level of implementation you decide.

We encourage educators to continue striving for a behavior (*growth*) mindset for students. It takes time to help students develop productive habits, as you have learned in this book. It will not happen overnight and requires intentionality and targetedness. It also requires us as adults to teach or reteach, model, and provide an environment for success for students and, most importantly, believe in the students we serve.

Students' brains do not fully develop until their approximate mid-twenties; they will have setbacks along the way and will need support to help learn from those setbacks and grow into empathic members in our respective communities. As educators, we must help teach or reteach students these targeted life skills and replacement behaviors they can utilize even when we are not there reminding them to do so. This gift (an inner toolkit of life skills) we give students through the implementation of behavior academies will be something they can utilize for the rest of their lives.

Follow the guidelines provided in this book and invest with sincere commitment, and you will no longer be able to go back to practices that have been deemed ineffective. We know better now, so we have to do better!

APPENDIX

This appendix includes a collection of reproducible tools referenced throughout this book. Use these tools along with the behavior rehearsal cards (accessible from www .solutiontree.com/free-resources/behavior/ba) to support your work with behavior academies.

Behavior Mindset Self-Inventory

1. Students should be punished when not demonstrating appropriate behaviors.

1	2	3	4	5
Strongly Disagree	Disagree	Neutral	Agree	Strongly Agree

2. Student behavior should be viewed as the communication of unmet needs and the absence of developed life skills and not taken personally.

1	2	3	4	5
Strongly Disagree	Disagree	Neutral	Agree	Strongly Agree

3. Someone other than myself should be teaching students appropriate behaviors (that is, their parents, school specialists, administrator, additional special services, and so on).

1	2	3	4	5
Strongly Disagree	Disagree	Neutral	Agree	Strongly Agree

4. Students need additional time and targeted support to learn appropriate replacement behaviors and receive opportunities to practice and generalize them.

1	2	3	4	5
Strongly Disagree	Disagree	Neutral	Agree	Strongly Agree

5. Exclusionary practices (that is, detention, suspensions, Saturday school, expulsions) will help improve a student's behavior.

1	2	3	4	5
Strongly Disagree	Disagree	Neutral	Agree	Strongly Agree

6. Students' behavior and life skills are developed over time with proper support.

1	2	3	4	5
Strongly Disagree	Disagree	Neutral	Agree	Strongly Agree

7. Student behavior is innate; therefore, additional targeted time, support, and practice will have a modest impact to improve their outcomes.

1	2	3	4	5
Strongly Disagree	Disagree	Neutral	Agree	Strongly Agree

8. Behavior interventions should provide targeted teaching and support of specific life skills.

1	2	3	4	5
Strongly Disagree	Disagree	Neutral	Agree	Strongly Agree

9. If student behavior doesn't improve right away, I feel frustrated and blame the intervention for being ineffective.

1	2	3	4	5
Strongly Disagree	Disagree	Neutral	Agree	Strongly Agree

10. I know improvement takes time, and I celebrate small wins with a student's behavior.

1	2	3	4	5
Strongly Disagree	Disagree	Neutral	Agree	Strongly Agree

11. I do not have time to teach or reteach students appropriate behavior.

1	2	3	4	5
Strongly Disagree	Disagree	Neutral	Agree	Strongly Agree

12. Ongoing feedback and support are critical to help with improving a student's behavior.

1	2	3	4	5
Strongly Disagree	Disagree	Neutral	Agree	Strongly Agree

13. Ongoing updates on a student's behavior progress are not important to me.

1	2	3	4	5
Strongly Disagree	Disagree	Neutral	Agree	Strongly Agree

14. I embrace the challenge of helping students learn appropriate behaviors.

1	2	3	4	5
Strongly Disagree	Disagree	Neutral	Agree	Strongly Agree

15. The majority of students receiving additional behavior interventions will not successfully respond to these supports at my school.

1	2	3	4	5
Strongly Disagree	Disagree	Neutral	Agree	Strongly Agree

page 2 of 4

16. At our school, we take collective responsibility for supporting a student's behavioral needs.

1	2	3	4	5
Strongly Disagree	Disagree	Neutral	Agree	Strongly Agree

17. There needs to be a special behavior program, classroom, or school within our district to which to send students who need extra help with behavior that provides the necessary time and space for them to learn.

1	2	3	4	5
Strongly Disagree	Disagree	Neutral	Agree	Strongly Agree

18. Setting realistic goals, progress monitoring them, and working through temporary student setbacks are essential to help improve academic behaviors, social behaviors, or both.

1	2	3	4	5
Strongly Disagree	Disagree	Neutral	Agree	Strongly Agree

19. There is no need to set goals or progress monitor since students will likely give up when they have a setback.

1	2	3	4	5
Strongly Disagree	Disagree	Neutral	Agree	Strongly Agree

20. Student voice is vital to improving student behavior.

1	2	3	4	5
Strongly Disagree	Disagree	Neutral	Agree	Strongly Agree

Behavior Mindset Self-Inventory Scoring

Total from odd numbers: _____   **Total from even numbers:** _____

Unproductive behavior mindset: Total from odd numbers in the 40- to 50-point range and total from even numbers in the 10- to 20-point range

An unproductive behavior mindset is a fixed mindset about student behavior. This type of educator believes students should already know how to demonstrate appropriate academic behaviors, social behaviors, or both. This educator believes that behavior is innate and that students would respond better through punishment than teaching. The unproductive mindset also believes that interventions are not worth the time or is the job of others to "fix" the student's behavior.

Undetermined behavior mindset: Total from odd numbers in the 21- to 39-point range and total from even numbers in the 21- to 39-point range

An undetermined behavior mindset is inconsistent beliefs about behavior. This type of educator believes some students can be taught appropriate academic behaviors, social behaviors, or both, and others cannot. While they may feel it is worth investing the time to support some students with their behavior, it should be someone else's job to provide it.

Productive behavior mindset: Total from odd numbers in the 10- to 20-point range and total from even numbers in the 40- to 50-point range

A productive behavior mindset is a growth mindset about student behavior. This type of educator believes that behavior is the communication of unmet needs and additional time, and targeted support will help students demonstrate and generalize appropriate academic behavior, social behavior, or both. This educator believes that behavior can be improved, and it is the collective responsibility of the school to provide the necessary support to ensure every student succeeds.

Scoring note: If the combination of your odd and even scoring ranges does not fall into a behavior mindset category, please consider the following: (1) retake the inventory to make sure you are not contradicting yourself in your ratings, or (2) consider yourself in the undetermined range due to the similarity of your scores supporting both productive and unproductive behavior mindset beliefs.

Behavior Academy Rubric—Lead Version

Behavior Academy Type:					
Behavior Academy Lead Name:					
Student in the Academy:					
Targeted Life Skills	**Minimal to No Mastery** Student inconsistently demonstrates or does not demonstrate (0)	**Emergent Mastery** Student demonstrates with prompt or cue (1)	**Internalized Mastery** Student independently demonstrates (2)	**Pre-Academy Score** Date: _____	**Post-Academy Score** Date: _____
Skill: _____					
Skill: _____					
Skill: _____					
Skill: _____					
Skill: _____					
Skill: _____					
Skill: _____					
Skill: _____					
Rubric mastery:	Rubric assessment mastery is 13–16 range by the end of the behavior academy. Rubric assessment mastery Met or Not Met = _____				
Notes and observations:				**Pre-Academy Total = ___**	**Post-Academy Total = ___**

Behavior Academy Rubric—Student Version

Academy Name:		
Student Name:		**Date:**
Life Skills	Define in your own words what each skill means. If you do not know, please write "I don't know."	*If you know what the skill means, how often would you say you utilize this skill? **Scale:** 1 = Never 2 = Rarely 3 = Sometimes 4 = Often 5 = Always
Skill: _____		Circle 1 2 3 4 5
Skill: _____		Circle 1 2 3 4 5
Skill: _____		Circle 1 2 3 4 5
Skill: _____		Circle 1 2 3 4 5
Skill: _____		Circle 1 2 3 4 5
Skill: _____		Circle 1 2 3 4 5
Skill: _____		Circle 1 2 3 4 5
Skill: _____		Circle 1 2 3 4 5
Rubric mastery:	Rubric assessment mastery is 32 or above range (80% or higher) by the end of the behavior academy. Rubric assessment mastery Met or Not Met = _____	
Notes and observations:		Pre-Academy Total = ____ Post-Academy Total = ____

Behavior Academy Attendance- and Goal-Monitoring Log

Student name:				
Behavior academy goal (or goals):				

	Attendance		Goal	
	Present	**Not Present**	**Met**	**Not Met**
Week 1	☐	☐	☐	☐
Week 2	☐	☐	☐	☐
Week 3	☐	☐	☐	☐
Week 4	☐	☐	☐	☐
Week 5	☐	☐	☐	☐
Week 6	☐	☐	☐	☐
Week 7	☐	☐	☐	☐
Week 8	☐	☐	☐	☐

Behavior Academy Ongoing Sessions Lesson Plan Template

1. Check-in and progress monitoring (five minutes)

Have students complete their self-monitoring form goal check-in with your supervision and guidance. Celebrate wins, and be prepared to help them navigate setbacks or barriers to success. Revisit previously learned session targeted skill and replacement behaviors: What skill and replacement behaviors did we learn during the last session?

2. Targeted lesson and skill rehearsal (ten to fifteen minutes)

Review the behavior rehearsal card skill focus definition and replacement behaviors.

Today's targeted life skill focuses of the session:	Skill definition in students' words after looking it up or discussing the definition with the students:
	What are some replacement behaviors to help demonstrate the targeted life skill focus (also provide one or two replacement behaviors)?

Behavior Rehearsal Card Session Scenario

Have students:

- Review the behavior rehearsal card scenario
- Say the skill focus and read the scenario
- Share the right way and wrong way to respond to the scenario
- Rehearse one or two of the taught replacement behaviors they can use to demonstrate the right way to respond if they were in that scenario

Student-Developed Scenario and Application

Help students:

- Come up with another similar scenario related to the focus area they may have experienced (if time permits)
- Develop the right way and wrong way to respond
- Rehearse one or two of the taught replacement behaviors they can use to demonstrate the right way to respond if they were in that scenario

3. Commitment and practice (five minutes)

Practice throughout the week: Help the student or students identify at least one targeted life skill (replacement behavior) to work on this week, and complete a written and/or verbal commitment to practice that identified life skill (replacement behavior).

Behavior Academy Student Progress-Monitoring Form—Older Students

Student name: _____ **Date:** _____

1 CHECK-IN AND PROGRESS MONITORING

Behavior academy goal:	Circle one: Met Partially Met Not Met
Behavior academy goal:	Circle one: Met Partially Met Not Met

What worked for you toward attaining your weekly goals?

What didn't work for you toward attaining your weekly goals?

Review: What was our skill focus last session? Review: What replacement behaviors did you learn to help you demonstrate this skill focus?	Were you able to apply the learned replacement behaviors successfully in any scenarios this past week? Explain.

2 TARGETED LESSON AND SKILL REHEARSAL

Today's skill focus of the session:	Skill definition:
	Replacement behaviors to help demonstrate the skill focus:

Behavior rehearsal card session scenario:	**Student-developed scenario and application:**
What is the skill focus?	What is another scenario about this skill focus you have experienced?
What is the right way to respond?	What is the right way to respond?
What is the wrong way to respond?	What is the wrong way to respond?
What is one replacement behavior that can help with the right way for this scenario?	What is one replacement behavior that can help with the right way for this scenario?

3 COMMITMENT AND PRACTICE

Practice throughout the week:

I _____ will work on _____ this week in order to meet my behavior goal (or goals).

Student signature: _____

page 2 of 2

Behavior Academy Student Progress-Monitoring Form—Younger Students

Student name: _____	**Date:** _____

How did I do this week? Circle one: ☺ ☐ ☹	Draw or explain why you circled the face you did.
Draw or write one thing you learned about the last time we met.	Today's new skill is _____. Draw or write what this skill looks like or sounds like. Draw or write one thing you can do to show this new skill.
New skill: What is the right way to respond?	New skill: What is the wrong way to respond?

I _____ will practice _____ this week.

Student signature: _____

Write "Your New Narrative" Individual Contract

Student name: _____ **Mentor or advisor name:** _____

Who am I?

_____

_____

_____

_____

What are some poor choices I have made in the past at school (my old narrative)?

_____

_____

_____

_____

What do I want to see for myself (my new narrative) when it comes to behavior and academics in school?

_____

_____

_____

_____

How do I plan on making this new narrative come true?

_____

_____

_____

_____

What help do I need to make this new narrative come true?

_____

_____

_____

_____

page 1 of 2

Who will I reach out to and how often to help make this new narrative come true?

_____

_____

_____

_____

What are my short-term goals toward this new narrative?

_____

_____

_____

_____

What are my long-term goals toward this new narrative?

_____

_____

_____

_____

My work toward my new narrative will begin on: _____

Student signature of commitment to my new narrative: _____

Check-In Commitment Schedule

Date: _____ Check-in with: _____ Commitments: _____ Initials: _____

Date: _____ Check-in with: _____ Commitments: _____ Initials: _____

Date: _____ Check-in with: _____ Commitments: _____ Initials: _____

Date: _____ Check-in with: _____ Commitments: _____ Initials: _____

Date: _____ Check-in with: _____ Commitments: _____ Initials: _____

Date: _____ Check-in with: _____ Commitments: _____ Initials: _____

Date: _____ Check-in with: _____ Commitments: _____ Initials: _____

Date: _____ Check-in with: _____ Commitments: _____ Initials: _____

Behavior Academy Planning Document

Who is leading the behavior academy: _____

Start date: _____

Scheduled delivery date, time, and frequency:

Once a week for twenty-five minutes: _____

Twice a week for twenty-five minutes: _____

Other: _____

Behavior Academy name:	Tactics to improve or maintain behavior academy structure:
☐ Hands-Off Academy	
☐ Check-In Check-Out Academy	
☐ Civility Academy	
☐ Organizational Skills Academy	
☐ Social Skills Academy	
☐ Upstander Academy	
☐ Motivation Academy	
☐ Emotional Regulation Academy	
Other: _____	
Other: _____	

Initial session planning components: introduction and purpose, preskills assessment, goal setting	
Introduction and purpose: What process will be utilized to introduce students to the purpose of the behavior academy?	
Preskills assessment: What targeted skills will be taught in this behavior academy? What method will be utilized to conduct a preskill assessment of these targeted skills in this behavior academy?	
Goal setting: What will the targeted goals be for this academy?	

page 1 of 2

Ongoing sessions planning components: check-in and progress monitoring, targeted lesson and skill rehearsal, commitment and practice	
Check-in and progress monitoring: What process or tool will be utilized to check-in and progress monitor with the students during each behavior academy session? How will you help students process through setbacks or barriers to success?	
Targeted lesson and skill rehearsal: What method or curricula will be utilized to teach and practice the targeted life skills aligned with the behavior academy in each session? What replacement behaviors will you be teaching in each ongoing session to help the student with the targeted skill focus?	
Commitment and practice: What process or tool will be utilized during each session to help students identify their commitment and practice skills prior to the next session?	
Exit session planning components: exit requirement, postskills assessment and goal mastery, commitment for ongoing success	
Exit requirement: What method or process will be utilized to demonstrate the behavior academy exit criterion is met?	
Postskills assessment and goal mastery: What method will be utilized to conduct a postskill assessment of the students in this behavior academy?	
Commitment for ongoing success: What method, process, or both will be utilized to ensure students who meet the exit requirement develop a commitment for ongoing success utilizing learned skills in the future?	

Build Your Own Behavior Academy Rehearsal Cards (Four Phases) Guide

Phase	Provide Evidence of This Phase
Phase 1: Name and define the behavior academy focus area based on student data.	Name of the behavior academy: Definition of the behavior academy: What data was utilized to decide this is a necessary behavior academy?
Phase 2: Identify and define the eight targeted life skills aligned with the behavior academy focus area.	List the eight targeted life skills aligned with the behavior academy: _____ _____ _____ _____ _____ _____ _____ _____ How did you identify the eight targeted life skills using the following three-pronged approach? Consider these questions as you determine your answer. 1. Did you collaborate with the teachers and other educators to capture the eight targeted life skills you want students to improve on? 2. Did you research the various life skills necessary for appropriately managing one's anger? 3. Did you leverage the collective expertise and experience in your building or district (staff who have a background or training in managing the behavior)?

Phase 3: Identify at least two replacement behaviors for each of the eight targeted life skills.	List the eight targeted life skills and two replacement behaviors for each life skill.

List the eight targeted life skills and two replacement behaviors for each life skill.

Life Skill: _____

Replacement Behavior 1: _____

Replacement Behavior 2: _____

Life Skill: _____

Replacement Behavior 1: _____

Replacement Behavior 2: _____

Life Skill: _____

Replacement Behavior 1: _____

Replacement Behavior 2: _____

Life Skill: _____

Replacement Behavior 1: _____

Replacement Behavior 2: _____

Life Skill: _____

Replacement Behavior 1: _____

Replacement Behavior 2: _____

Life Skill: _____

Replacement Behavior 1: _____

Replacement Behavior 2: _____

Life Skill: _____

Replacement Behavior 1: _____

Replacement Behavior 2: _____

Life Skill: _____

Replacement Behavior 1: _____

Replacement Behavior 2: _____

How did you decide on the replacement behaviors for each of the eight targeted life skills?

What will you be utilizing to teach the replacement behaviors (imagery and visualization exercises, existing lessons from behavior curriculum or resources your school has, creating your own, and so on)?

Phase 4: Develop a rehearsal application scenario aligned with each of the eight targeted life skills.	List the eight targeted skills. Insert a short scenario for application practice next to each:

List the eight targeted skills. Insert a short scenario for application practice next to each:

Life Skill: _____

Scenario: _____

Life Skill: _____

Scenario: _____

Life Skill: _____

Scenario: _____

Life Skill: _____

Scenario: _____

Life Skill: _____

Scenario: _____

Life Skill: _____

Scenario: _____

Life Skill: _____

Scenario: _____

Life Skill: _____

Scenario: _____

How did you create the scenarios?

Behavior Rehearsal Card Template

Front of Behavior Rehearsal Card	Back of Behavior Rehearsal Card
Definition:	*Rehearsal and application scenario:*
Replacement behaviors:	Wrong way to respond? Right way to respond?
	Student-created scenario:
	Wrong way to respond? Right way to respond?

Targeted life skill:

Academy

Sample Behavior Academy Permission Slip Template

Student's name: _____

Behavior academy name and description: _____

Behavior academy lead and contact information: _____

Behavior academy rationale:

_____

_____

_____

_____

_____

Starting date: _____   Ending date: _____ (TBD based on data)

I give permission for this behavior academy to be implemented.

Parent or guardian signature: _____   Date: _____

Targeted Intervention Teacher and Stakeholder Input Survey

Please complete this rating based on your perceptions and observations with the student this week. Remember to please rate based on the behavior focus (life skills) we have been focusing on in the behavior academy.

Student name: _____

Rate progress: _____

3 = Making progress

2 = Minimal progress

0 = No progress

Explain your rating in a few sentences:

Behavior Academy Session At-a-Glance

Student name:	Behavior academy lead:	Date:
Mark (X) targeted life skill session focus	Hands-Off Academy targeted life skills	Ways a teacher or stakeholder can help:

Behavior Academy Matching Sheet (BAM-S)

	Strongly Agree (3)	Agree (2)	Sometimes Agree (1)	Disagree (0)	Strongly Disagree (0)
1. Student struggles to calm down when angry or perceiving an unfair situation (HOA).					
2. Student responds to adult attention and feedback (CICOA).					
3. Student struggles with civil discourse with peers (CA).					
4. Student is often behind with classwork (OSA).					
5. Student struggles to develop and maintain peer relationships (SSA).					
6. Student is often involved in social problems between students or groups of students (UA).					
7. Student appears to not care about school (MA).					
8. Student experiences intense emotions (ERA).					
9. Student utilizes his or her hands when upset or angered (HOA).					
10. Student responds to structure and check-ins (CICOA).					
11. Student is often engaged in verbal disagreements with peers or adults (CA).					
12. Student is overwhelmed with classwork (OSA).					
13. Student is not included by peers (SSA).					
14. Student gives in quickly to peer pressure (UA).					
15. Student has limited to no sense of connectedness or belonging at school (MA).					
16. Student struggles to self-regulate (ERA).					

page 1 of 2

	Strongly Agree (3)	Agree (2)	Sometimes Agree (1)	Disagree (0)	Strongly Disagree (0)
17. Student struggles with impulse control and conflict resolution (HOA).					
18. Student responds to wins throughout the day (CICOA).					
19. Student struggles to see other perspectives (CA).					
20. Student may respond to goal setting and prioritizing (OSA).					
21. Student may benefit from learning how to engage with peers appropriately (SSA).					
22. Student struggles with problem solving and empathy (UA).					
23. Student struggles with self-concept (MA).					
24. Student shuts down or acts out for a prolonged time when triggered (ERA).					

Behavior Academy	Items	Sum Score (A sum score of 6 or higher may be a behavior academy to consider.)
Hands-Off Academy (HOA)	1, 9, 17	
Check-In Check-Out Academy (CICOA)	2, 10, 18	
Civility Academy (CA)	3, 11, 19	
Organizational Skills Academy (OSA)	4, 12, 20	
Social Skills Academy (SSA)	5, 13, 21	
Upstander Academy (UA)	6, 14, 22	
Motivation Academy (MA)	7, 15, 23	
Emotional Regulation Academy (ERA)	8, 16, 24	

REFERENCES

Clear, J. (2018). *Atomic habits: Tiny changes, remarkable results—an easy and proven way to build good habits and break bad ones.* New York: Penguin Random House.

Commonwealth of Virginia. (2022, November 7). *Pandemic impact on public K–12 education: Report to the governor and the general assembly of Virginia.* Richmond, VA: Commonwealth of Virginia and Review Commission. Accessed at https://jlarc.virginia.gov/pdfs/reports/Rpt568-1.pdf on September 21, 2023.

Dweck, C. S. (2017). *Mindset: The new psychology of success* (Updated ed.). New York: Ballantine Books.

Hannigan, J., Hannigan, J. D., Mattos, M., & Buffum, A. (2021). *Behavior solutions: Teaching academic and social skills through RTI at Work.* Bloomington, IN: Solution Tree Press.

Ji, J. L., Kavanagh, D. J., Holmes, E. A., MacLeod, C., & Di Simplicio, M. (2019). Mental imagery in psychiatry: Conceptual and clinical implications. *CNS Spectrums, 24*(1), 114–126. Accessed at https://cambridge.org/core/services/aop-cambridge-core/content/view/9B72ED99BA371CC60D7CE5C5417AE673/S1092852918001487a.pdf/div-class-title-mental-imagery-in-psychiatry-conceptual-and-clinical-implications-div.pdf on September 21, 2023.

National Center for Education Statistics. (2022, July 6). *More than 80 percent of U.S. public schools report pandemic has negatively impacted student behavior and socio-emotional development.* Accessed at https://nces.ed.gov/whatsnew/press_releases/07_06_2022.asp on September 21, 2023.

Wong, H. K., & Wong, R. T. (2018). *The first days of school: How to be an effective teacher* (5th ed.). Author.

INDEX

Behavior Solutions
John Hannigan, Jessica Djabrayan Hannigan, Mike Mattos,
and Austin Buffum
Take strategic action to close the systemic behavior gap with Behavior Solutions.
This user-friendly resource outlines how to utilize the PLC at Work® and
RTI at Work™ processes to create a three-tiered system of supports that is
collaborative, research-based, and practical.
BKF891

Taking Action
Austin Buffum, Mike Mattos, and Janet Malone
This comprehensive implementation guide covers every element required to
build a successful RTI at Work™ program in schools. The authors share step-
by-step actions for implementing the essential elements, the tools needed to
support implementation, and tips for engaging and supporting educators.
BKF684

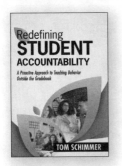

Redefining Student Accountability
Tom Schimmer
The time has come to separate academic achievement from student behavior.
Learn a three-tiered framework, as well as trauma-informed, restorative,
and schoolwide approaches to teaching responsibility, nurturing student
accountability, and addressing student behavior to support student ownership in
the classroom.
BKG002

Up to the Challenge
Jay Jackson
This timely resource lets educators take a deep dive into helping students build
character to confront and overcome challenges. With passion and purpose,
author Jay Jackson blends personal challenges and achievements to equip
teachers with tools to improve student resilience.
BKG076

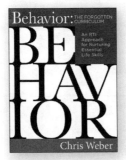

Behavior: The Forgotten Curriculum
Chris Weber
Discover how to fully prepare students for college, careers, and life by nurturing
their behavioral skills along with their academic skills. Learn how to employ the
most effective behavioral-skill exercises for your particular class and form unique
relationships with every learner.
BKF828

"WOW!

I liked how I was given
an effective, organized plan
to help EVERY child."

—Linda Rossiter, teacher,
Spring Creek Elementary School, Utah

 PD Services

Our experts draw from decades of research and their own experiences to bring you
practical strategies for providing timely, targeted interventions. You can choose from a
range of customizable services, from a one-day overview to a multiyear process.

Book your RTI PD today!
888.763.9045

Solution Tree